Women in the Old Testament

Women
in the
Old Testament

Irene Nowell, O.S.B.

A Liturgical Press Book

THE LITURGICAL PRESS
Collegeville, Minnesota

Cover design by Ann Blattner. "Judith" by Botticelli.

6   7   8

Library of Congress Cataloging-in-Publication Data

Nowell, Irene, 1940–
  Women in the Old Testament / Irene Nowell.
    p.   cm.
  Includes bibliographical references.
  ISBN 0-8146-2411-1
    1. Women in the Bible.   2. Bible.   O.T.—Biography.   I. Title.
  BS575.N64   1997
  221.9'22'082—dc21   97-2358
                                                CIP

Contents

Introduction

Stories are a gift to the imagination. They help us imagine people and places and experiences different from our own. They help us imagine the realities of our own lives in different terms. Biblical stories also help us imagine the relationship of God with human beings. They give us words to describe our own relationship with God.

It is only in recent years that attention has been given to the stories of biblical women. The growing awareness of women's stories has revealed a rich variety. There are stories of queens and slaves, assassins and victims of rape, mothers and wives, sisters and in-laws. Each of these women has unique characteristics. Each of these stories is food for our imaginations.

The Bible has also provided us with stories of what it means to be a woman created in the image of God, and stories of God portrayed in the image of a woman.

This book tells the stories of only some of the women in the Old Testament. It is hoped that the introduction to their stories will encourage readers to search for more biblical women and also to find the story of faith reflected in the stories of their own lives.

1. Women of Israel's Beginnings

Suggested Readings: Genesis 12; 15–17; 18:1-15; 21–23.

SARAH

Sarah is the wife of Abraham, God's first covenant partner.[1] Her first appearance is in the genealogy of Terah, Abraham's father (Gen 11:27-32). There we learn that she is the wife of Abraham, that she is barren, and that she has traveled with Terah and his family from Ur to Haran. These three elements—her husband, her barrenness, her traveling—will weave through her whole story.

THE JOURNEY

Genesis 12:4-5

> [4]Abram went as the LORD directed him, and Lot went with him. Abram was seventy-five years old when he left Haran. [5]Abram took his wife Sarai, his brother's son Lot, all the possessions that they had accumulated, and the persons they had acquired in Haran, and they set out for the land of Canaan.

Abraham is called by God to leave his home and family and to go to a new land. God promises that he will be blessed and that all nations will find blessing in him (Gen 12:1-3). Abraham obeys without a word, taking everything that belongs to him. Sarah is mentioned only as accompanying Abraham. We are reduced to speculation about her.

---

[1]Note that Abraham and Sarah first appear with variant names: Abram and Sarai.

Abraham is 75 years old. By a process of deduction—Sarah is ten years younger than Abraham in Gen 17:17—we can assume that when she leaves Haran she is 65. Two of the threads which weave through her story are already evident in these two verses. She is a faithful wife to Abraham and she is again traveling. She, too, leaves home and family at the command of the God who speaks to Abraham. She believes in Abraham who believes in God. She will be essential to God's fulfillment of the promises to Abraham, and through Abraham to all nations.

The rabbinic tradition speculates on what Sarah did for the ninety years while she was barren. It is said that she taught the other women about the one God. Because of the significance of her spiritual leadership, Abraham always set up her tent first.[2] In a patriarchal society it is rare to find such primary consideration given to women. The tradition highlights the unique importance of Sarah to whom even the great father Abraham defers.

WIFE-SISTER STORIES

Genesis 12:10-20

[10]There was famine in the land; so Abram went down to Egypt to sojourn there, since the famine in the land was severe. [11]When he was about to enter Egypt, he said to his wife Sarai: "I know well how beautiful a woman you are. [12]When the Egyptians see you, they will say, 'She is his wife'; then they will kill me, but let you live. [13]Please say, therefore, that you are my sister, so that it may go well with me on your account and my life may be spared for your sake." [14]When Abram came to Egypt, the Egyptians saw how beautiful the woman was; and when Pharaoh's courtiers saw her, [15]they praised her to Pharaoh. So she was taken into Pharaoh's palace. [16]On her account it went very well with Abram, and he received flocks and herds, male and female slaves, male and female asses, and camels.

[2]R. Huniah, "Abraham converted the men and Sarah the women" (Parashah 39:14.1 on Gen 12:5); R. Haninah, "The word is so written as to be read, 'his tent.' Once he had pitched Sarah's tent, he pitched his own" (Parashah 39:15.5 on Gen 12:8). Jacob Neusner, *Genesis Rabbah: The Judaic Commentary to the Book of Genesis. A New American Translation* (Brown Judaic Studies 105; Atlanta: Scholars Press, 1985) 2.74.

¹⁷But the LORD struck Pharaoh and his household with severe plagues because of Abram's wife Sarai. ¹⁸Then Pharaoh summoned Abram and said to him: "How could you do this to me! Why didn't you tell me she was your wife? ¹⁹Why did you say, 'She is my sister,' so that I took her for my wife? Here, then, is your wife. Take her and be gone!"

²⁰Then Pharaoh gave men orders concerning him, and they sent him on his way, with his wife and all that belonged to him.

Abraham does not remain long in Canaan. Because of a famine in the land he moves on to Egypt. There Sarah, and with her the promise of descendants, is endangered by being taken into the harem of Pharaoh. The reason for her endangerment seems to be Abraham's claim that she is his sister.

The basic plot of the wife-sister story appears three times (Gen 12:10-20; 20:1-18; 26:6-11). In each story the patriarch is afraid that someone will kill him in order to marry his beautiful wife. Therefore he tells the ruler of the land that his wife is his sister.

Two of these three stories are about Abraham and Sarah. In Genesis 12 we learn first of all that Sarah is beautiful. It is important to note that almost no one is described as beautiful in the Bible who is not also holy.³ So there is an implication that Sarah is not only beautiful; she is also holy. She is not only beautiful; she is *very* beautiful. Abraham's perception of her is confirmed by the Egyptians. Pharaoh's courtiers praise Sarah to Pharaoh. Is this woman who is very beautiful also very holy?

Sarah holds life and death. Abraham is afraid that he will be killed because of her. So he wants her to claim to be his sister so that "it may go well with [him] on her account and [his] life may be spared for her sake." Abraham is right. Not only is his life spared; it goes very well with him and he is made wealthy because of her. Pharaoh's life is also in Sarah's hands. Because she is endangered, all living things in Pharaoh's house are threatened. He and his household are struck with

³See Joseph (Gen 39:6), David (1 Sam 16:12), Tamar (2 Sam 13:1), Abishag (1 Kings 1:3-4).

severe plagues. When she is returned to Abraham, the plagues depart from Pharaoh's house. His plight foreshadows that of a later pharaoh who will be struck with plagues so that Sarah's descendants might be delivered from slavery (Exod 7:14–12:30).

The other wife-sister story (Gen 20:1-18) is similar. The king is Abimelech of Gerar. He discovers that Sarah is Abraham's wife through a dream in which God comes to him and says, "You are about to die because of the woman you have taken, for she has a husband" (20:3). Death and life are again in her hands. Abimelech is threatened with death and told to "return the man's wife," so that his life might be spared. When Abimelech summons Abraham, he defends himself by claiming that he thought he would be killed because of Sarah.

In this second story, God defends Sarah even when Abraham does not. "God had tightly closed every womb in Abimelech's household on account of Abraham's wife Sarah" (20:18). Sarah, the barren woman, brings barrenness to Abimelech's household. When she is restored to her husband, God restores health to Abimelech's "wife and his maidservants, so that they could bear children."

Not only God is concerned about Sarah's honor. Abimelech is also concerned. After he gives gifts to Abraham, he says to Sarah, "See, I have given your brother a thousand shekels of silver. Let that serve you as a vindication [literally, a covering of the eyes] before all who are with you; your honor has been preserved with everyone" (20:16).

In spite of Abraham apparently disowning her, Sarah is identified throughout both stories as his wife. She is called Abraham's wife six times in each story (12:11, 12, 17, 18, 19, 20; 20:2, 7, 11, 12, 14, 18). She remains barren. God has protected her from other men, but she still waits to bear her husband's child. The two passages continue the story of her travels. She goes with Abraham to Egypt and to Gerar.

DESCENDANTS

Genesis 17:15-22

15God further said to Abraham: "As for your wife Sarai, do not call her Sarai; her name shall be Sarah. 16I will bless her, and I will give you a son by her. Him also will I bless; he shall give rise to nations, and rulers of peoples shall issue from him." [17]Abraham prostrated himself and laughed as he said to himself, "Can a child be born to a man who is a hundred years old? Or can Sarah give birth at ninety?" [18]Then Abraham said to God, "Let but Ishmael live on by your favor!" [19]God replied: "Nevertheless, your wife Sarah is to bear you a son, and you shall call him Isaac. I will maintain my covenant with him as an everlasting pact, to be his God and the God of his descendants after him. [20]As for Ishmael, I am heeding you: I hereby bless him. I will make him fertile and will multiply him exceedingly. He shall become the father of twelve chieftains, and I will make of him a great nation. [21]But my covenant I will maintain with Isaac, whom Sarah shall bear to you by this time next year." [22]When he had finished speaking with him, God departed from Abraham.

The stories in Genesis 15–17 circle around the two poles of God's covenant promise to Abraham of descendants, and Sarah's continued childlessness. In Genesis 15, God promises Abraham descendants as many as the stars. Abraham has complained that, since he has no children, his servant Eliezer will be his heir. God reassures him, "your own issue shall be your heir" (15:4).

Sarah, however, is still barren and so she decides to give her servant Hagar to her husband Abraham so in that way she might give him sons (16:1-6). In doing this she is following the Mesopotamian custom for a barren wife. The practice, which is described in law codes from Nuzi, was an ancient form of surrogate motherhood. The child born to the servant was to be considered the child of the wife. In the case of Sarah and Hagar this does not work. Sarah never claims Hagar's child. In fact, she eventually drives out both mother and child.

The incident with Hagar portrays the dark side of Sarah. After Hagar becomes pregnant, Sarah accuses Abraham of causing the conflict in the household. Abraham passes the responsibility back to Sarah, who abuses Hagar so much that she runs away. At the command of God's angel Hagar returns only to be expelled again by her jealous mistress after the birth of Sarah's child. In her relationship with Hagar, Sarah appears cruel and ruthless.

In Genesis 17 God renews the covenant with Abraham and promises again that Abraham will be "the father of a host of nations" (17:4). Abraham thinks now that this promise will be fulfilled through Ishmael, Hagar's son (cf. 17:18). But God tells him that it is Sarah who will be the mother of the child of promise (17:16). Abraham's response is laughter. He cannot believe that he can beget a child at one hundred years of age or that Sarah can give birth at ninety (17:17). God, however, will not be stopped. God has protected Sarah throughout the wife-sister episodes and now reassures Abraham that the promise will come through Sarah. Not only Abraham is blessed in this chapter; not only Abraham has a formal naming, a sign of blessing (17:5-6). Sarah is blessed; Sarah is given a name (17:15-16). God promises, "I will bless her. She will give rise to nations and rulers of peoples will issue from her." (17:16).[4] Sarah is identified as the mother of the covenant and recipient of the covenant promises along with her husband Abraham.

ANNOUNCEMENT OF BIRTH

Genesis 18:1-15

> [1]The LORD appeared to Abraham by the terebinth of Mamre, as he sat in the entrance of his tent, while the day was growing hot. [2]Looking up, he saw three men standing nearby. When he saw them, he ran from the entrance of the tent to greet them; and bowing to the ground, [3]he said: "Sir, if I may ask you this favor, please do not go on past your servant. [4]Let some water be brought, that you may bathe your feet, and then rest yourselves under the tree. [5]Now that you have come this close to your servant, let me bring you a little food, that you may refresh yourselves; and afterward you may go on your way." "Very well," they replied, "do as you have said."

> [6]Abraham hastened into the tent and told Sarah, "Quick, three seahs of fine flour! Knead it and make rolls." [7]He ran to the herd, picked out a tender, choice steer, and gave it to

[4]The NAB follows the Greek translation (the Septuagint) here which says that Ishmael will be blessed and give rise to nations and kings. The Hebrew text applies these promises to Sarah.

a servant, who quickly prepared it. [8]Then he got some curds and milk, as well as the steer that had been prepared, and set these before them; and he waited on them under the tree while they ate.

[9]"Where is your wife Sarah?" they asked him. "There in the tent," he replied. [10]One of them said, "I will surely return to you about this time next year, and Sarah will then have a son." Sarah was listening at the entrance of the tent, just behind him. [11]Now Abraham and Sarah were old, advanced in years, and Sarah had stopped having her womanly periods. [12]So Sarah laughed to herself and said, "Now that I am so withered and my husband is so old, am I still to have sexual pleasure?" [13]But the LORD said to Abraham: "Why did Sarah laugh and say, 'Shall I really bear a child, old as I am?' [14]Is anything too marvelous for the LORD to do? At the appointed time, about this time next year, I will return to you, and Sarah will have a son." [15]Because she was afraid, Sarah dissembled, saying, "I didn't laugh." But he said, "Yes you did."

Three visitors come to Abraham and Sarah. After Abraham takes care of the needs of hospitality and they are fed with Sarah's help, one of them asks: "Where is your wife Sarah?" "There in the tent," Abraham replies. It seems that when male guests were being entertained, it was proper for the female members of the family to remain out of sight. Sarah, however, is not out of earshot. She is at the door of the tent, listening to the whole conversation.

The guest continues, "I will surely return to you about this time next year, and Sarah will then have a son." In this version of the story it is Sarah who laughs, well aware that she is no longer able to conceive. The visitor, however, also seems capable of hearing the conversation on both sides of the tent flap. He says, "Why did Sarah laugh? Is anything too marvelous for the LORD to do?" The promise is renewed once more: Sarah will have a son. Sarah is afraid of this stranger who knows so much. She lies, saying, "I did not laugh." The stranger, however, is not deceived. "Yes you did!"

By this time in the story attention has shifted from three visitors to one visitor and that visitor has been identified as God. This story is yet another renewal of God's covenant promise that Abraham will have descendants, that they will be his own children, and that they will be the children of Sarah. The announcement of birth found in Genesis 17 and 18 follows a form found frequently in biblical texts.[5] The major parts of the form are:

1. Appearance of the Lord or an angel of the Lord (cf. 17:1; 18:1).
2. Expression of fear or reverence by the human being (cf. 17:3; 18:2).
3. The message (cf. 17:16; 18:10):
   a. A woman is pregnant and will bear a son.
   b. The son's name shall be . . . .
   c. The future of the child will be . . . .
4. Objection by the human being (cf. 17:17-18; 18:12).
5. Reassurance by God or the angel (cf. 17:19-21; 18:13-14).
6. The gift of a sign.

In the two stories, Genesis 17 and 18, there are two important omissions from the form. First of all, the child's name is given only in the reassurance. His name will be Isaac (*yishaq*), which means "he laughs." The name is suggested in both announcement stories. The objection in both stories is laughter: Abraham laughs in 17:17; Sarah laughs in 18:12. Secondly, there is no sign given in either story. In Genesis 17, circumcision is given as a sign of the covenant; in Genesis 18, the extraordinary knowledge of the visitor might be construed as a sign. Or perhaps the child himself is to be seen as a sign, not only of the truth of the announcement story but also of God's fidelity to the covenant promise.

There are two stories of the announcement of Isaac's birth because the story was preserved in two traditions. The final editors of the Pentateuch (Genesis–Deuteronomy) kept as much of the tradition as they could, even if stories repeated or

[5]The form appears several times: announcements of the birth of Ishmael (Gen 16:7-12); Isaac (Gen 17:1-3, 15-21; 18:1-15); of Samson (Judg 13:2-24). The passage most familiar to Christians is the announcement of the birth of Jesus (Luke 1:26-38); see also the birth of John the Baptist (Luke 1:8-23).

contradicted each other. The story in Genesis 18 is from a tenth-century tradition called the Yahwist source because of its preference for the name "Yahweh" (Lord) for God. The story in Genesis 17 is from a sixth-century tradition called the Priestly source because it is commonly believed that the priests during the Babylonian exile collected these stories and wrote them down.

The two announcement stories reveal that Sarah, as well as Abraham, is chosen by God. She is the mother of the promise. Sarah is capable and still works hard at the tasks of hospitality even when she is ninety years old. Sarah has a lively sense of humor and a strong dose of reality. She also knows fear and succumbs to deceit when the stranger quizzes her concerning her laughter. She is a strong woman and a complex character.

SARAH AND HER SON

Genesis 21:1-8

[1]The LORD took note of Sarah as he had said he would; he did for her as he had promised. [2]Sarah became pregnant and bore Abraham a son in his old age, at the set time that God had stated. [3]Abraham gave the name Isaac to this son of his whom Sarah bore him. [4]When his son Isaac was eight days old, Abraham circumcised him, as God had commanded. [5]Abraham was a hundred years old when his son Isaac was born to him. [6]Sarah then said, "God has given me cause to laugh, and all who hear of it will laugh with me. [7]Who would have told Abraham," she added, "that Sarah would nurse children! Yet I have borne him a son in his old age." [8]Isaac grew, and on the day of the child's weaning, Abraham held a great feast.

"The LORD took note of Sarah as . . . promised. Sarah became pregnant and bore Abraham a son" (21:1-2). Sarah is specifically named as the one who receives the promise. Sarah, who complained that God kept her from bearing children (Gen 16:2), now recognizes that it is through God that her child is born. Her response bears witness again to her sense of humor and her ability to laugh at herself. Now she says, "God has given me cause to laugh." Sarah also knows her own part in this happy event. "I have borne [Abraham] a son in his old age." God and Sarah have given Abraham a son, the child of promise.

Sarah's struggles are not over, however. Sarah notices Ishmael, Hagar's son, playing with Isaac and demands of Abraham: "Drive out that slave and her son" (Gen 21:10). Surprisingly God tells a distressed Abraham, "Heed the demands of Sarah, no matter what she is asking of you; for it is through Isaac that descendants shall bear your name" (Gen 21:12). God is still taking note of Sarah, even though it seems that her importance is overshadowed by that of her son. Abraham, the father of God's covenant people, is instructed to obey his wife Sarah.

Sarah, who seems overly protective of Isaac in the story of Ishmael, is absent from the story of Abraham's near sacrifice of her son (Gen 22:1-19). We are reduced again to speculation. Is it Sarah who must let go of this son to whom she is so fiercely attached? Did Abraham tell Sarah his purpose when the two left for Mount Moriah? What did Isaac say to his mother when they returned?

It seems strangely significant that the next mention we have of Sarah is the report of her death (Gen 23:1-2). The span of her life was 127 years; according to this Priestly text she lived almost forty years after the birth of Isaac. Abraham mourns for her according to custom and then sets out to find a place for her burial. He buys the cave of Machpelah near Hebron from the Hittites and buries her there. When he dies he is buried there with her (Gen 25:9) and eventually Isaac and Rebekah, Jacob and Leah will also be buried there. The burial cave is the only land ever owned by Abraham, this man who was promised land, descendants, and a special relationship with God. Sarah is significant in the fulfillment of all God's promises to Abraham.

The final note about Sarah returns to the important relationship between mother and son. Isaac takes his new wife into the tent of his mother Sarah and, in his love for Rebekah, finds comfort after Sarah's death (Gen 24:67).

WHO IS SARAH?

Sarah is wife to Abraham, sharing in all his travels, his trials, and God's covenant promises to him. After ninety years of barrenness, she becomes the mother of Isaac, the covenant child. She begins a long line of barren women who mother children of promise: Rebekah, Rachel, Hannah, mother of Samuel; Elizabeth, mother of John the Baptist. The line comes to its ultimate fullness in a woman who, although remaining a virgin, also becomes a mother. Through the power of God's spirit, Mary gives birth to the child who is hope for all of us. Is anything impossible to God? Like Mary, Sarah is also a model of the church who mothers the people of God. Paul tells Christians: "You . . . are children of the promise . . . children not of the slave woman [Hagar] but of the freeborn woman [Sarah]" (Gal 4:28, 31).

HAGAR

MAID OF SARAH

Genesis 16:1-6

1Abram's wife Sarai had borne him no children. She had, however, an Egyptian maidservant named Hagar. 2Sarai said to Abram: "The LORD has kept me from bearing children. Have intercourse, then, with my maid; perhaps I shall have sons through her." Abram heeded Sarai's request. 3Thus, after Abram had lived ten years in the land of Canaan, his wife Sarai took her maid, Hagar the Egyptian, and gave her to her husband Abram to be his concubine. 4He had intercourse with her, and she became pregnant. When she became aware of her pregnancy, she looked on her mistress with disdain. 5So Sarai said to Abram: "You are responsible for this outrage against me. I myself gave my maid to your embrace; but ever since she became aware of her pregnancy, she has been looking on me with disdain. May the LORD decide between you and me!" 6Abram told Sarai: "Your maid is in your power. Do to her whatever you please." Sarai then abused her so much that Hagar ran away from her.

Hagar is the "maid of Sarah" (Gen 16:8), an Egyptian (16:1). Is she one of "the persons" Abraham had acquired in Haran (Gen 12:5)? She appears first by name in Genesis 16 when Sarah decides to use her as a surrogate mother in order to give sons to Abraham. Sarah says, "I shall have sons through her." Through the first three verses of this chapter

Hagar is the object of others' actions: Sarah had a maid; Sarah gave Hagar to Abraham; he had intercourse with her. For a fleeting moment she becomes the subject: She became pregnant; she became aware of her pregnancy; she looked on her mistress with disdain. But Sarah does not allow Hagar to take her place for long. She complains to Abraham who says, "Your maid is in your power." Sarah then abuses Hagar so much that she runs away.

The incident, however, has given Hagar a certain status. Although the New American Bible translates her role as "concubine" (16:3), literally she is given to Abraham "to be his wife."[6] As a second wife she has certain rights, particularly in consequence of her pregnancy.

The ancient law code of Hammurabi (18th century B.C.E.) provides a context by which to understand Sarah's giving of her maid to her husband. There is precedent for a barren wife using a slave as a surrogate mother. Sarah's complaint against Hagar is also clarified by this law code. The slave who bears the master's children may not consider herself to have the same legal standing as the wife.[7] Even so, the wife may not sell the slave. But may she drive her out? Is Hagar still a slave or is she a wife?

VISION IN THE DESERT

Genesis 16:7-16

> [7]The LORD's messenger found her by a spring in the wilderness, the spring on the road to Shur, [8]and he asked, "Hagar maid of Sarai, where have you come from and where are you going?" She answered, "I am running away from my mistress, Sarai." [9]But the LORD's messenger told her: "Go back to your mistress and submit to her abusive treatment. [10]I will make your descendants so numerous," added the LORD's messenger, "that they will be too many to count. [11]Besides," the LORD's messenger said to her:

[6]She is called in Hebrew *'ishshah*, "wife," rather than *pilegesh*, "concubine."

[7]Hammurabi, §144–§146. See Victor H. Matthews and Don C. Benjamin, *Old Testament Parallels: Laws and Stories from the Ancient Near East* (New York: Paulist, 1991) 64–65.

"You are now pregnant and shall bear a son;
  you shall name him Ishmael,
For the LORD has heard you,
  God has answered you.

12 He shall be a wild ass of a man,
  his hand against everyone,
  and everyone's hand against him;
In opposition to all his kin
  shall he encamp."

13To the LORD who spoke to her she gave a name, saying, "You are the God of Vision"; she meant, "Have I really seen God and remained alive after my vision?" 14That is why the well is called Beer-lahai-roi. It is between Kadesh and Bered.

15Hagar bore Abram a son, and Abram named the son whom Hagar bore him Ishmael. 16Abram was eighty-six years old when Hagar bore him Ishmael.

The fleeing Hagar meets a messenger of God, an angel of the Lord. First the messenger asks her a powerful question: "Hagar, maid of Sarai, where have you come from and where are you going?" (16:8). She answers truthfully, "I am running away from my mistress Sarai" (16:8). However, she has no answer concerning where she is going. The messenger gives the difficult answer to that question: "Return to your mistress."

But the messenger has another message for Hagar. The central elements of the announcement of birth form (see above p. 10) are easily recognized:

1. The appearance of an angel of the Lord (16:7).
3. The message (16:11-12).
   a. Hagar is pregnant and will bear a son (16:11).
   b. The son's name shall be Ishmael, "God hears" (16:11).
   c. The future of the child will be strife (16:12).

The form is abbreviated. There is no expression of fear or reverence (#2) nor is there an objection (#4). Therefore, there is no need for either reassurance (#5) or sign (#6). It must be noted, however, that this is the first time in the Bible that the form appears.

Hagar is the first person to be visited by an angel. She is the first to hear an announcement of birth. She is the first woman to bear a child in the story of the ancestors (Gen 12–50). She is promised descendants in the same terms that such promises are given to male ancestors (Gen 16:10; cf. Gen 15:5; 17:5-6; 22:16; 26:4; 28:14).

Hagar is the only person in the Bible to give a name to God: "To the LORD who spoke to her she gave a name, saying, 'You are the God of Vision'" (Gen 16:13). In all of Hagar's story, only God, whether in person or through a messenger, speaks to Hagar. Only God calls her by name. (Sarah and Abraham consistently call her "maid" or "slave.") It is God who sees Hagar as a person, hears her, sends a messenger to her, names her, makes her mother of a nation. Hagar in turn sees God as a person and gives a name to God: ʾel-roʾi, "the God who sees."

Hagar returns to the house of Abraham and bears him a son according to the angel's promise. Abraham (instead of Hagar) names this firstborn son the name that the angel had given him, Ishmael, which is interpreted, "God hears." Abraham is eighty-six years old at the time of Ishmael's birth. How old is Hagar?

EXPULSION

Genesis 21:9-13

> 9Sarah noticed the son whom Hagar the Egyptian had borne to Abraham playing with her son Isaac; 10so she demanded of Abraham: "Drive out that slave and her son! No son of that slave is going to share the inheritance with my son Isaac!" 11Abraham was greatly distressed, especially on account of his son Ishmael. 12But God said to Abraham: "Do not be distressed about the boy or about your slave woman. Heed the demands of Sarah, no matter what she is asking of you; for it is through Isaac that descendants shall bear your name. 13As for the son of the slave woman, I will make a great nation of him also, since he too is your offspring."

After the birth of Isaac (Gen 21:1-8), Sarah is intent that everything—wealth, attention, blessing—will go to her son. "No son of *that slave* is going to share the inheritance with my son Isaac" (21:10, emphasis mine). The sight of Ishmael playing with Isaac is enough cause for her to demand that Abraham once more expel Hagar along with her son.[8]

Sarah demands that Abraham expel Hagar and Ishmael. Abraham is initially unwilling, "especially on account of his son Ishmael." Hagar's value has diminished now that she has borne Abraham a son. God, however, has not forgotten her. "Do not be distressed about the boy *or about your slave woman*" (21:12, emphasis mine). But even God's attention has moved elsewhere. God reminds Abraham that it is Sarah who mothers the child of promise. As an afterthought, God promises nations to Ishmael because he is *Abraham's* offspring. Hagar has virtually disappeared.

There are some legal implications to this incident. The Deuteronomic law code (7th century B.C.E.) states:

> If a man with two wives loves one and dislikes the other; and if both bear him sons, but the first-born is of her whom he dislikes: when he comes to bequeath his property to his sons he may not consider as his first-born the son of the wife he loves, in preference to his true first-born, the son of the wife whom he dislikes. On the contrary, he shall recognize as his first-born the son of her whom he dislikes, giving him a double share of whatever he happens to own, since he is the first fruits of his manhood, and to him belong the rights of the first-born (Deut 21:15-17).

The inheritance rights of the child of a slave are described in the code of Hammurabi:

> If a citizen who has children by his wife and by his slave adopts the slave's children, his estate shall be divided evenly between the children of both, after his wife's first-born son receives the preferential share (cf. Gen 21:9-21).[9]

[8]The Hebrew text says simply that she saw Ishmael "playing." The phrase "with her son Isaac" is missing from the Hebrew but is found in the Septuagint (Greek) and in the Vulgate (Latin). A pun may cast light on Sarah's difficulty. Ishmael's "play" is *mesaheq* in Hebrew, from the same root *(shq)* as Isaac's name. Ishmael is "Isaac-ing." In no way is Sarah going to allow Ishmael to take Isaac's place, even in "play."

[9]Hammurabi §170. See Matthews and Benjamin, 66.

Several questions arise regarding the status of Hagar and of her son Ishmael. Is Hagar Abraham's second wife as Gen 16:3 implies? If so, the later Deuteronomic law code protects against abuses such as Abraham's against Hagar and Ishmael. Is Hagar simply the slave who is surrogate mother? Hammurabi's law would have required Abraham to grant Ishmael part of the inheritance, since he has certainly adopted him. Abraham names him (Gen 16:15), claims him (17:18), is concerned for him (21:11). Even in the ancient world the treatment of Hagar is against the law as well as against human compassion.

DESERT REVISITED

Genesis 21:14-21

> [14]Early the next morning Abraham got some bread and a skin of water and gave them to Hagar. Then, placing the child on her back, he sent her away. As she roamed aimlessly in the wilderness of Beer-sheba, [15]the water in the skin was used up. So she put the child down under a shrub, [16]and then went and sat down opposite him, about a bowshot away; for she said to herself, "Let me not watch to see the child die." As she sat opposite him, he began to cry. [17]God heard the boy's cry, and God's messenger called to Hagar from heaven: "What is the matter, Hagar? Don't be afraid; God has heard the boy's cry in this plight of his. [18]Arise, lift up the boy and hold him by the hand; for I will make of him a great nation." [19]Then God opened her eyes, and she saw a well of water. She went and filled the skin with water, and then let the boy drink.
>
> [20]God was with the boy as he grew up. He lived in the wilderness and became an expert bowman, [21]with his home in the wilderness of Paran. His mother got a wife for him from the land of Egypt.

Hagar wanders again in the desert. The supplies provided by Abraham run out and both Hagar and her son face death. She places the child at a distance in order not to see him die. Then she begins to cry.[10] It is, however, the boy's voice that

---

[10]The Hebrew text says that "she" cried (Gen 21:16). The Septuagint, perhaps harmonizing with v. 17, says that "he" cried.

God hears. The angel of God returns and renews the promise that Ishmael will grow into a great nation. Then this woman of vision sees again. "God opened her eyes, and she saw a well of water" (21:19).

Hagar and her son remain in the desert. The story continues to focus on Ishmael. God is with him. His mother gets a wife for him from Egypt, her homeland. Ishmael lives to a ripe old age and becomes the father of twelve tribes (Gen 25:12-18). They are listed as enemies of the twelve tribes of Israel: "The tents of Ishmael and Edom, / the people of Moab and Hagar" (Ps 83:7). They are without the wisdom that belongs to Israel: "The sons of Hagar who seek knowledge on earth, / the merchants of Midian and Teman, / the phrasemakers seeking knowledge, / These have not known the way to wisdom, / nor have they her paths in mind" (Bar 3:23).

WHO IS HAGAR?

In the beginning of the story Hagar is called *shiphah*, "maid" (Gen 16:1, 2, 3, 5, 6, 8; cf. 25:12). Sarah gives her to Abraham as a wife, *'ishshah* (Gen 16:3). When Sarah drives her out with Ishmael, she refers to Hagar as "slave," *'amah* (Gen 21:10, 12, 13).

The tension in the story may turn on the struggle between Hagar's roles. Is Hagar the surrogate mother and is her son therefore to be considered the son of Sarah? Or is Hagar the wife who bears the first-born to Abraham? Is Ishmael to be considered Abraham's first-born son with the rights of the first-born? Is he the son of a slave woman, who does not have the rights of the first-born, but does have a right to inherit? This tension may explain Hagar's disdainful attitude toward Sarah and Sarah's abuse of Hagar (Gen 16:6). It may also explain Sarah's fear that Ishmael will inherit along with Isaac (Gen 21:10). Hagar's status may have improved with her pregnancy and childbearing, but her situation certainly has not.

Nonetheless, Hagar is a significant person in the ancestor story. She is intimately involved with the covenant promise to Abraham of descendants. She is a woman of vision. She sees and names God; she sees God's gifts and providence. Although she is not part of the ongoing history of God's covenant people, the stories concerning her seem to be told from her viewpoint. Although powerless as female, slave, and foreigner, she becomes the mother of a nation.

Yet Hagar remains the outcast. In Christian tradition, she (the foreign woman) becomes ironically the symbol of Judaism, the old covenant, and Sarah (the mother of the Jewish people) becomes the symbol of Christianity: "Now this is an allegory. These women represent two covenants. One was from Mount Sinai, bearing children for slavery; this is Hagar. Hagar represents Sinai, a mountain in Arabia; it corresponds to the present Jerusalem, for she is in slavery along with her children" (Gal 4:24-25). In this allegory Paul is using strong language to contrast Judaism with Christianity. He describes Judaism as if it were enslaved to an over-literal interpretation of the law and Christianity as set free by Christ. His point is that the true law for both Jews and Christians is the law of love: "In Christ Jesus, neither circumcision nor uncircumcision counts for anything, but only faith working through love" (Gal 5:6). Hagar suffers yet again in comparison to Sarah. She is the symbol of slavery; Sarah, the symbol of freedom. Yet it is only in the reconciliation of their children that all the descendants of Abraham will be able to rejoice in God's kingdom.

2. More Women of Israel's Beginnings

Suggested Readings: Genesis 24; 25:19-34; 26:6-11; 27:1-46; 28:1-5; 29:1-35; 30:1-43; 31:14-35; 34; 35:16-20; 38.

REBEKAH

BETROTHAL

Rebekah is the daughter of Bethuel and granddaughter of Abraham's brother Nahor and his wife Milcah (Gen 22:23). She becomes the wife of Isaac, the son of Abraham and Sarah, the child of promise.

The story of Rebekah's betrothal to Isaac (Genesis 24) is one of the longest chapters in Scripture. The narrative is a type scene, a literary convention in which the narrator is expected to include a specific set of elements as the story is told. The set of expected elements for the betrothal type scene include: a stranger, a well, a young woman, haste, drawing water, sharing a meal. All the expected elements are found in Genesis 24.

Abraham, interested in the continuation of God's promise through descendants, sends his servant back to Mesopotamia to find a wife for Isaac (24:1-9). When the servant expresses some fear, Abraham assures him, "God will send his messenger before you and you will obtain a wife for my son there."

Genesis 24:10-14

¹⁰The servant then took ten of his master's camels, and bearing all kinds of gifts from his master, he made his way to the city of Nahor in Aram Naharaim. ¹¹Near evening, at the time when women go out to draw water, he made the camels kneel by the well outside the city. ¹²Then he prayed: "LORD, God of my master Abraham, let it turn out favorably for me

today and thus deal graciously with my master Abraham. 13While I stand here at the spring and the daughters of the townsmen are coming out to draw water, 14if I say to a girl, 'Please lower your jug, that I may drink,' and she answers, 'Take a drink, and let me give water to your camels, too,' let her be the one whom you have decided upon for your servant Isaac. In this way I shall know that you have dealt graciously with my master."

When the servant arrives in Mesopotamia, he sets up a test for God. If the young woman is generous, strong, and reliant, then she is the right one for Isaac. Thus this is to be a marriage made in heaven. God decides who the bride will be. God's choice of this woman is a sign of God's covenant love (in Hebrew, *hesed*) for Isaac (24:14). Marriage is one of the Bible's favorite images for the covenant between God and the people. Just as Isaac is a sign of God's covenant with Abraham, so his wife will be a sign of God's faithful covenant love.

Genesis 24:15-33

15He had scarcely finished these words when Rebekah (who was born to Bethuel, son of Milcah, the wife of Abraham's brother Nahor) came out with a jug on her shoulder. 16The girl was very beautiful, a virgin, untouched by man. She went down to the spring and filled her jug. As she came up, 17the servant ran toward her and said, "Please give me a sip of water from your jug." 18"Take a drink, sir," she replied, and quickly lowering the jug onto her hand, she gave him a drink. 19When she had let him drink his fill, she said, "I will draw water for your camels, too, until they have drunk their fill." 20With that, she quickly emptied her jug into the drinking trough and ran back to the well to draw more water, until she had drawn enough for all the camels. 21The man watched her the whole time, silently waiting to learn whether or not the LORD had made his errand successful. 22When the camels had finished drinking, the man took out a gold ring weighing half a shekel, which he fastened on her nose, and two gold bracelets weighing ten shekels, which he put on her wrists. 23Then he asked her: "Whose daughter are you? Tell me, please. And is there room in your father's house for us to spend the night?" 24She answered: "I am the daughter of Bethuel the son of Milcah, whom she bore to

Nahor. ²⁵There is plenty of straw and fodder at our place," she added, "and room to spend the night." ²⁶The man then bowed down in worship to the LORD, ²⁷saying: "Blessed be the LORD, the God of my master Abraham, who has not let his constant kindness toward my master fail. As for myself also, the LORD has led me straight to the house of my master's brother."

²⁸Then the girl ran off and told her mother's household about it. ²⁹Now Rebekah had a brother named Laban. ³⁰As soon as he saw the ring and the bracelets on his sister Rebekah and heard her words about what the man had said to her, Laban rushed outside to the man at the spring. When he reached him, he was still standing by the camels at the spring. ³¹So he said to him: "Come, blessed of the LORD! Why are you staying outside when I have made the house ready for you, as well as a place for the camels?" ³²The man then went inside; and while the camels were being unloaded and provided with straw and fodder, water was brought to bathe his feet and the feet of the men who were with him. ³³But when the table was set for him, he said, "I will not eat until I have told my tale." "Do so," they replied.

These verses are characterized by haste. The servant has scarcely finished speaking when Rebekah arrives. She offers the servant a drink and quickly lowers her jug to give him water. She offers to water the camels, quickly empties the jug, and runs back and forth to the well until the camels are satisfied. All this time the servant watches her work, waits to see if she passes the test.

After the camels are watered, the servant gives her gold jewelry and asks her name. He is amazed that God has not only provided this generous and energetic young woman, but that she is one of Abraham's relatives. In these early stories, belonging to the same family or clan as the groom is an asset for the bride.

Rebekah offers the servant hospitality: "There is plenty of straw and fodder at our place and room to spend the night." Then she runs to tell her family. Her brother Laban, after he has seen the gold, runs to meet the stranger. The servant is in a hurry, too. He will not eat until he has accomplished his errand.

The servant tells his story (Gen 24:34-48), repeating most of the details (one reason this chapter is so long), and states: "If, therefore, you have in mind to show true loyalty to my master, let me know; but if not, let me know that, too. I can then proceed accordingly" (24:49). Laban replies: "This thing comes from the LORD; we can say nothing to you either for or against it. Here is Rebekah, ready for you; take her with you, that she may become the wife of your master's son, as the LORD has said" (24:50-51). The servant is eager to be off, but the family, in typical middle-Eastern fashion, urges the servant to stay and celebrate for ten days (24:52-54). Who will get to decide? Her brother and mother call Rebekah and ask her, "Do you wish to go with this man?" and she answers, "I do" (24:58). Apparently they know that Rebekah makes up her own mind. The marriage, as is customary, is decided by the men. But the departure time is decided by the bride.

Genesis 24:59-67

[59]At this they allowed their sister Rebekah and her nurse to take leave, along with Abraham's servant and his men. [60]Invoking a blessing on Rebekah, they said:

> "Sister, may you grow
>   into thousands of myriads;
> And may your descendants gain possession
>   of the gates of their enemies!"

[61]Then Rebekah and her maids started out; they mounted their camels and followed the man. So the servant took Rebekah and went on his way.

[62]Meanwhile Isaac had gone from Beer-lahai-roi and was living in the region of the Negeb. [63]One day toward evening he went out . . . in the field, and as he looked around, he noticed that camels were approaching. [64]Rebekah, too, was looking about, and when she saw him, she alighted from her camel [65]and asked the servant, "Who is the man out there, walking through the fields toward us?" "That is my master," replied the servant. Then she covered herself with her veil.

[66]The servant recounted to Isaac all the things he had done. [67]Then Isaac took Rebekah into his tent; he married her, and thus she became his wife. In his love for her Isaac found solace after the death of his mother Sarah.

The family invokes a blessing on Rebekah. This is the first story in Genesis that tells of one human being blessing another. It is fitting that the one blessed should be Rebekah. She will be instrumental in the next blessing scene.

A touching story closes the chapter. As the travelers arrive at their destination Rebekah spies Isaac walking toward them. She ascertains his identity and with becoming modesty covers herself with her veil. Isaac takes her into his mother's tent,[1] and in his love for her, Isaac finds solace after the death of his mother.

Rebekah is a worthy daughter-in-law of Sarah. She is a beautiful woman, strong, generous, and willing to work. She is a woman of decision, capable of acting on the decision at the moment. She is willing, as Abraham and Sarah were, to leave homeland and family. She leaves, not only for a land she has never seen, but for a husband she has never seen. She is a brave woman. God has chosen a husband for her and she runs to accomplish her part. God has chosen a good wife for Isaac, child of promise.

DESCENDANTS

Genesis 25:19-26

[19]This is the family history of Isaac, son of Abraham; Abraham had begotten Isaac. [20]Isaac was forty years old when he married Rebekah, the daughter of Bethuel the Aramean of Paddan-aram and the sister of Laban the Aramean. [21]Isaac entreated the LORD on behalf of his wife, since she was sterile. The LORD heard his entreaty, and Rebekah became pregnant. [22]But the children in her womb jostled each other so much that she exclaimed, "If this is to be so, what good will it do me!" She went to consult the LORD, [23]and he answered her:

> "Two nations are in your womb,
>   two peoples are quarreling while still within you;
> But one shall surpass the other,
>   and the older shall serve the younger."

[1]The Hebrew of Gen 24:67 reads: "Isaac brought her into the tent of his mother Sarah." It is sometimes emended to read "into his tent."

24When the time of her delivery came, there were twins in her womb. 25The first to emerge was reddish, and his whole body was like a hairy mantle; so they named him Esau. 26His brother came out next, gripping Esau's heel; so they named him Jacob. Isaac was sixty years old when they were born.

Again we have the story of a barren wife whose child is to be the child of promise. Rebekah, however, conceives twins: Esau, the hairy elder, and Jacob, the crafty younger. The struggle between the two begins in the womb. Rebekah is as decisive with God as she is in human encounters. She herself goes to seek God's word. She complains, "If this is to be so, what good will it do me!" God hears her complaint and answers her. The response does not alleviate her physical distress, but explains its reason. The two children are really two nations, the people of Edom and the people of Israel (cf. Gen 25:30; 32:29). The twins' struggle represents the struggle of nations. A final note indicates that Isaac prefers Esau while Rebekah prefers Jacob (25:28). The parents' preferences seem insignificant, but the blessing scene will prove otherwise.

WIFE-SISTER STORY

Genesis 26:6-11

6So Isaac settled in Gerar. 7When the men of the place asked questions about his wife, he answered, "She is my sister." He was afraid, if he called her his wife, the men of the place would kill him on account of Rebekah, since she was very beautiful. 8But when he had been there for a long time, Abimelech, king of the Philistines, happened to look out of a window and was surprised to see Isaac fondling his wife Rebekah. 9He called for Isaac and said: "She must certainly be your wife! How could you have said, 'She is my sister'?" Isaac replied, "I thought I might lose my life on her account." 10"How could you do this to us!" exclaimed Abimelech. "It would have taken very little for one of the men to lie with your wife, and you would have thus brought guilt upon us!" 11Abimelech therefore gave this warning to all his men: "Anyone who molests this man or his wife shall forthwith be put to death."

This is the third wife-sister story. The two preceding stories (Gen 12:10-20; 20:1-18) concern Sarah and Abraham. The plot is similar in all three stories. There are some significant variations, however, in this third story. First of all, Rebekah is younger in the story than Sarah, thus heightening the danger to her husband. Secondly, Abimelech (cf. Gen 20:1-18) discovers the deception in a much more natural fashion. He sees the husband fondling the wife. Thirdly, the Hebrew word for "fondling" is *mesaheq*, from the same root as Isaac's name *(yishaq)*, a root which means "laughter, play."[2] There is a pun in the story: Abimelech sees Isaac "isaacking" his wife.

If we consider the three wife-sister stories in Genesis, we see Rebekah suffering the same humiliation as Sarah. Both women are denied by their husbands. Rebekah is described again as very beautiful (cf. Gen 24:16). She, like Sarah, holds life and death.

BLESSING

Genesis 27:5-13

> [5]Rebekah had been listening while Isaac was speaking to his son Esau. So when Esau went out into the country to hunt some game for his father, [6]Rebekah said to her son Jacob, "Listen! I overheard your father tell your brother Esau, [7]'Bring me some game and with it prepare an appetizing dish for me to eat, that I may give you my blessing with the LORD's approval before I die.' [8]Now, son, listen carefully to what I tell you. [9]Go to the flock and get me two choice kids. With these I will prepare an appetizing dish for your father, such as he likes. [10]Then bring it to your father to eat, that he may bless you before he dies." [11]"But my brother Esau is a hairy man," said Jacob to his mother Rebekah, "and I am smooth-skinned! [12]Suppose my father feels me? He will think I am making sport of him, and I shall bring on myself a curse instead of a blessing." [13]His mother, however, replied: "Let any curse against you, son, fall on me! Just do as I say. Go and get me the kids."

As the story of the *birth* of Isaac is primary for Sarah, the story of the *blessing* of Jacob is the most significant passage

[2]Compare Gen 21:9 where Ishmael is "playing" *(mesaheq)*.

concerning Rebekah. In this passage she, not Isaac, makes the decision concerning which son will continue as God's covenant partner. Rebekah herself was blessed by her mother and brother (cf. Gen 24:60). In her initial appearance in the biblical narrative she shows herself quick and strong-minded (24:18-20, 58). She prefers Jacob to Esau (25:28). She has heard God's word that the elder will serve the younger (25:23). Her action will confirm the choice.

Rebekah, having overheard Isaac's plan to bless Esau (Gen 27:1-4), concocts a plan to substitute Jacob for the favored son. She, who should know her husband, will prepare a meal that Isaac likes. (The appetizing meal is mentioned three times: 27:9, 14, 17!) She, who knows her sons, will disguise Jacob as Esau (cf. 27:15-16). When Jacob is afraid that his father will discover him and give him a curse instead of a blessing, his mother Rebekah says, "Let any curse against you, son, fall on me!" She will sacrifice anything for her beloved son.

Rebekah's plan succeeds. Isaac, initially suspicious, is reassured and blesses Jacob with a wonderful blessing. When Esau comes with his appetizing dish, he is too late. All he can get is a half-hearted blessing which amounts to a curse.

MOTHER AND SONS

Genesis 27:41-46

> [41]Esau bore Jacob a grudge because of the blessing his father had given him. He said to himself, "When the time of mourning for my father comes, I will kill my brother Jacob." [42]When Rebekah got news of what her older son Esau had in mind, she called her younger son Jacob and said to him: "Listen! Your brother Esau intends to settle accounts with you by killing you. [43]Therefore, son, do what I tell you: flee at once to my brother Laban in Haran, [44]and stay with him a while until your brother's fury subsides [45][until your brother's anger against you subsides] and he forgets what you did to him. Then I will send for you and bring you back. Must I lose both of you in a single day?"

> [46]Rebekah said to Isaac: "I am disgusted with life because of the Hittite women. If Jacob also should marry a Hittite woman, a native of the land, like these women, what good would life be to me?"

In Rebekah's final scene she is protecting her younger son from her elder son. Not surprisingly, Esau is ready to kill Jacob because of the blessing. Equally predictable, Rebekah solves the problem indirectly. She proposes to Isaac that Jacob go back to Haran to find a wife. To Jacob, however, she explains the planned journey clearly as flight from the murderous Esau. Isaac follows Rebekah's suggestion and sends Jacob back to the house of Bethuel. As Jacob departs, Isaac blesses him again, this time with full recognition (Gen 28:1-5).

Rebekah does not see her favored son again. Her death is not reported, but she is not mentioned when Jacob finally returns to the house of Isaac (Gen 35:27). She and Isaac are buried in Hebron (the cave in Machpelah) with Abraham and Sarah (Gen 49:31). It was demanded of Abraham that he sacrifice his son; it was demanded of Rebekah, too, that she give up her beloved son. Rebekah married the child of promise; she mothered and chose the child of blessing.

LEAH AND RACHEL

BETROTHAL

Genesis 29:9-14

> 9While [Jacob] was still talking with [the shepherds], Rachel arrived with her father's sheep; she was the one who tended them. 10As soon as Jacob saw Rachel, the daughter of his uncle Laban, with the sheep of his uncle Laban, he went up, rolled the stone away from the mouth of the well, and watered his uncle's sheep. 11Then Jacob kissed Rachel and burst into tears. 12He told her that he was her father's relative, Rebekah's son, and she ran to tell her father. 13When Laban heard the news about his sister's son Jacob, he hurried out to meet him. After embracing and kissing him, he brought him to his house. Jacob then recounted to Laban all that had happened, 14and Laban said to him, "You are indeed my flesh and blood."

The story of Jacob's meeting with Rachel is another betrothal type scene.[3] Most of the elements are present: a stranger,

---

[3]See discussion of Genesis 24 above.

a young woman, a well, drawing water, a sense of haste. The variations in the story reveal Jacob's passionate nature. At the sight of Rachel, he alone rolls the massive stone from the mouth of the well. Then he kisses his cousin and bursts into tears. It is indeed a story of love at first sight!

TWO SISTERS

Genesis 29:14-20

> After Jacob had stayed with him a full month, [15]Laban said to him: "Should you serve me for nothing just because you are a relative of mine? Tell me what your wages should be." [16]Now Laban had two daughters; the older was called Leah, the younger Rachel. [17]Leah had lovely eyes, but Rachel was well formed and beautiful. [18]Since Jacob had fallen in love with Rachel, he answered Laban, "I will serve you seven years for your younger daughter Rachel." [19]Laban replied, "I prefer to give her to you rather than to an outsider. Stay with me." [20]So Jacob served seven years for Rachel, yet they seemed to him but a few days because of his love for her.

Jacob's love for Rachel makes him willing to serve Laban seven years for her, a generous bride-price. But the years seem as nothing because of the strength of his passion.

The description of Laban's two daughters suggests the description of Rebekah's two sons (Gen 25:27-28). The two are named: Leah, meaning "wearied," and Rachel, meaning "ewe." They are identified as elder and younger.

Again we are given more information than seems necessary. The added information, however, is crucial for the plot of the story. We are told that Rachel is "well formed and beautiful," confirming the reasons for Jacob's love. There is something noteworthy, however, about Leah's eyes. The word describing them, *rakkoth*, means "tender," "gentle," "frail," "delicate," "weak."[4] It has sometimes been interpreted as meaning weak or watery eyes; it is sometimes translated as

---

[4]See for example the calf in Gen 18:7; the children in Gen 33:13; the man and woman in Deut 28:54, 56; words in Prov 15:1 and 25:15.

"lovely."[5] It has been suggested that perhaps Leah had blue eyes, a strange occurrence in the Middle East. It is well known that blue eyes are more sensitive to light, thus watery, and are often myopic. They can certainly also be lovely!

MARRIAGE

Genesis 29:21-30

> [21]Then Jacob said to Laban, "Give me my wife, that I may consummate my marriage with her, for my term is now completed." [22]So Laban invited all the local inhabitants and gave a feast. [23]At nightfall he took his daughter Leah and brought her to Jacob, and Jacob consummated the marriage with her. [24](Laban assigned his slave girl Zilpah to his daughter Leah as her maidservant.) [25]In the morning Jacob was amazed: it was Leah! So he cried out to Laban: "How could you do this to me! Was it not for Rachel that I served you? Why did you dupe me?" [26]"It is not the custom in our country," Laban replied, "to marry off a younger daughter before an older one. [27]Finish the bridal week for this one, and then I will give you the other too, in return for another seven years of service with me."
>
> [28]Jacob agreed. He finished the bridal week for Leah, and then Laban gave him his daughter Rachel in marriage. [29](Laban assigned his slave girl Bilhah to his daughter Rachel as her maidservant.) [30]Jacob then consummated his marriage with Rachel also, and he loved her more than Leah. Thus he remained in Laban's service another seven years.

The story of Jacob's marriage to Rachel and Leah is a story of the deceiver deceived. Jacob, the younger brother, schemed to steal the blessing from Esau, the elder. Jacob serves Laban seven years to marry Rachel, the younger sister, and instead is given Leah, the elder. Rachel cost him another seven years.

---

[5]The translations show the confusion: Septuagint, *astheneis* (weak); Vulgate, *lippis* (inflamed or watery); Douay, bleary-eyed; KJV, tender-eyed; RSV, weak; JB, no sparkle; NEB, dull-eyed; NAB, lovely. Some of the newer translations use "lovely": NJB, NRSV. However, JPS translates "weak," and REB stays with NEB "dull-eyed."

The story may be poetic justice for Jacob. One can only imagine the sorrow and pain it presents to the two sisters. Leah can have no doubt that her husband loves her sister more. Rachel suffers the indignity of seeing her sister celebrate and consummate what was to be her own marriage with a man who loves her passionately. The seeds of strife are planted between the two sisters and they seem powerless to change the course of events.

DESCENDANTS

Genesis 29:31–30:13

31When the LORD saw that Leah was unloved, he made her fruitful, while Rachel remained barren. 32Leah conceived and bore a son, and she named him Reuben; for she said, "It means, 'The LORD saw my misery; now my husband will love me.'" 33She conceived again and bore a son, and said, "It means, 'The LORD heard that I was unloved,' and therefore he has given me this one also"; so she named him Simeon. 34Again she conceived and bore a son, and she said, "Now at last my husband will become attached to me, since I have now borne him three sons"; that is why she named him Levi. 35Once more she conceived and bore a son, and she said, "This time I will give grateful praise to the LORD"; therefore she named him Judah. Then she stopped bearing children.

30:1When Rachel saw that she failed to bear children to Jacob, she became envious of her sister. She said to Jacob, "Give me children or I shall die!" 2In anger Jacob retorted, "Can I take the place of God, who has denied you the fruit of the womb?" 3She replied, "Here is my maidservant Bilhah. Have intercourse with her, and let her give birth on my knees, so that I too may have offspring, at least through her." 4So she gave him her maidservant Bilhah as a consort, and Jacob had intercourse with her. 5When Bilhah conceived and bore a son, 6Rachel said, "God has vindicated me; indeed he has heeded my plea and given me a son." Therefore she named him Dan. 7Rachel's maidservant Bilhah conceived again and bore a second son, 8and Rachel said, "I engaged in a fateful struggle with my sister, and I prevailed." So she named him Naphtali.

⁹When Leah saw that she had ceased to bear children, she gave her maidservant Zilpah to Jacob as a consort. ¹⁰So Jacob had intercourse with Zilpah, and she conceived and bore a son. ¹¹Leah then said, "What good luck!" So she named him Gad. ¹²Then Leah's maidservant Zilpah bore a second son to Jacob; ¹³and Leah said, "What good fortune!"—meaning, "Women call me fortunate." So she named him Asher.

Gen 29:31–30:24 chronicles the struggle between the two sisters, Leah and Rachel, over who can give birth to Jacob's children. Leah is fruitful but unloved; Rachel is loved but barren. Leah gives birth to four sons: Reuben, Simeon, Levi, and Judah. In despair Rachel demands of Jacob: "Give me children or I shall die!" Jacob, in hot anger, retorts: "Can I take the place of God?" So Rachel turns to the same solution that Sarah tried, surrogate motherhood through her maidservant Bilhah. After Bilhah bears two sons for Rachel, Dan and Naphtali, Leah also gives her maidservant Zilpah to Jacob. Zilpah also bears two sons for Leah: Gad and Asher.

The mothers' interpretations of their sons' names indicate the progress of the struggle between the two sisters. Leah's first four sons are named Reuben (the LORD saw my misery), Simeon (the LORD heard that I was unloved), Levi (now my husband will become attached to me), Judah (I will give grateful praise). Rachel's sons through Bilhah are Dan (God has vindicated me) and Naphtali (I have wrestled with my sister and prevailed). Leah responds with the names of her sons through Zilpah: Gad (what good luck!) and Asher (women call me fortunate).

Genesis 30:14-24

¹⁴One day, during the wheat harvest, when Reuben was out in the field, he came upon some mandrakes which he brought home to his mother Leah. Rachel asked Leah, "Please let me have some of your son's mandrakes." ¹⁵Leah replied, "Was it not enough for you to take away my husband, that you must now take my son's mandrakes too?" "Very well, then!" Rachel answered. "In exchange for your son's mandrakes, Jacob may lie with you tonight." ¹⁶That evening, when Jacob came home from the fields, Leah went

out to meet him. "You are now to come in with me," she told
him, "because I have paid for you with my son's mandrakes." So that night he slept with her, [17]and God heard her
prayer; she conceived and bore a fifth son to Jacob. [18]Leah
then said, "God has given me my reward for having let my
husband have my maidservant"; so she named him
Issachar. [19]Leah conceived again and bore a sixth son to
Jacob; [20]and she said, "God has brought me a precious gift.
This time my husband will offer me presents, now that I
have borne him six sons"; so she named him Zebulun.
[21]Finally, she gave birth to a daughter, and she named her
Dinah.

[22]Then God remembered Rachel; he heard her prayer and
made her fruitful. [23]She conceived and bore a son, and she
said, "God has removed my disgrace." [24]So she named him
Joseph, meaning, "May the LORD add another son to this one
for me!"

Still the contest continues. Rachel has access to Jacob because he loves her; Leah is still ahead in the number of sons.
So the sisters make a bargain. Rachel trades a night with Jacob
for mandrakes which Leah's son has gathered. Mandrakes
were considered a fertility drug in the ancient world. The bargain suggests cooperation between the two sisters although
the sharp language reveals the tension between them.

The trade seems to work for both sisters. Leah gives birth
to Issachar (God has given me my reward) and subsequently
to Zebulun (my husband will offer me presents). Leah now
has six sons of her own and two through Zilpah. Finally God
remembers Rachel. She, too, gives birth to a son, her firstborn,
whom she names Joseph (may the Lord add another). Rachel
now has one son of her own and two through Bilhah. Her sister has prevailed in the struggle. Eight of Jacob's eleven sons
are Leah's; only three are Rachel's. Leah has more than her
share of the twelve future tribes.

DEPARTURE FROM HARAN

Meanwhile, as the sisters struggle with each other, Jacob
struggles with Laban for wealth. No matter what terms Laban
sets, Jacob wins. "Thus the man grew increasingly prosperous,

and he came to own not only large flocks but also male and female servants and camels and asses" (Gen 30:43). Laban's sons are not happy with Jacob's increasing prosperity. The fourteen years of service are long over. So Jacob sends for Rachel and Leah and reports to them the tension between himself and Laban and his sons. He also tells them of a dream in which God commands him to return to the land of his birth.

Genesis 31:14-35

¹⁴Rachel and Leah answered him: "Have we still an heir's portion in our father's house? ¹⁵Are we not regarded by him as outsiders? He not only sold us; he has even used up the money that he got for us! ¹⁶All the wealth that God reclaimed from our father really belongs to us and our children. Therefore, do just as God has told you." ¹⁷Jacob proceeded to put his children and wives on camels, ¹⁸and he drove off with all his livestock and all the property he had acquired in Paddan-aram, to go to his father Isaac in the land of Canaan.

¹⁹Now Laban had gone away to shear his sheep, and Rachel had meanwhile appropriated her father's household idols. ²⁰Jacob had hoodwinked Laban the Aramean by not telling him of his intended flight. ²¹Thus he made his escape with all that he had. Once he was across the Euphrates, he headed for the highlands of Gilead.

²²On the third day, word came to Laban that Jacob had fled. ²³Taking his kinsmen with him, he pursued him for seven days until he caught up with him in the hill country of Gilead. ²⁴But that night God appeared to Laban the Aramean in a dream and warned him, "Take care not to threaten Jacob with any harm!"

²⁵When Laban overtook Jacob, Jacob's tents were pitched in the highlands; Laban also pitched his tents there, on Mount Gilead. ²⁶"What do you mean," Laban demanded of Jacob, "by hoodwinking me and carrying off my daughters like war captives? ²⁷Why did you dupe me by stealing away secretly? You should have told me, and I would have sent you off with merry singing to the sound of tambourines and harps. ²⁸You did not even allow me a parting kiss to my daughters and grandchildren! What you have now done is a

senseless thing. ²⁹I have it in my power to harm all of you; but last night the God of your father said to me, 'Take care not to threaten Jacob with any harm!' ³⁰Granted that you had to leave because you were desperately homesick for your father's house, why did you steal my gods?" ³¹"I was frightened," Jacob replied to Laban, "at the thought that you might take your daughters away from me by force. ³²But as for your gods, the one you find them with shall not remain alive! If, with my kinsmen looking on, you identify anything here as belonging to you, take it." Jacob, of course, had no idea that Rachel had stolen the idols.

³³Laban then went in and searched Jacob's tent and Leah's tent, as well as the tents of the two maidservants; but he did not find the idols. Leaving Leah's tent, he went into Rachel's. ³⁴Now Rachel had taken the idols, put them inside a camel cushion, and seated herself upon them. When Laban had rummaged through the rest of her tent without finding them, ³⁵Rachel said to her father, "Let not my lord feel offended that I cannot rise in your presence; a woman's period is upon me." So, despite his search, he did not find his idols.

Rachel and Leah are as willing to leave family and homeland as were Sarah and Rebekah. So they and their children and maidservants depart with Jacob to return to Canaan. Rachel, however, has stolen her father's household idols, thus removing the symbols of Laban's authority. Laban's pursuit of Jacob seems to be motivated primarily by the loss of the household gods. Jacob, innocent of the theft, pledges that the culprit will die and Laban searches the tents of all the women. Rachel, however, has hidden the idols in a camel cushion and is sitting on them. She apologizes for not standing when her father enters; her excuse is her menstrual period. So Laban does not find the gods and makes peace with the departing Jacob.

Rachel's reasons for stealing the household idols are never stated. Is it her way of getting even with the father who so long ago denied her the wedding night? Is it her claim to Laban's property? In any case, she proves herself as adept at deceiving her male relatives as her aunt Rebekah. Her claim of menstrual discomfort, whether true or not, subtly declares the uncleanness of the idols. Anything on which a menstruating woman sits is made unclean and anyone who touches anything on which she sits is also made unclean (Lev 15:19-24). Idols are unclean by definition. Rachel's action underlines that fact.

BIRTH AND DEATH

Genesis 35:16-20

16Then they departed from Bethel; but while they still had some distance to go on the way to Ephrath, Rachel began to be in labor and to suffer great distress. 17When her pangs were most severe, her midwife said to her, "Have no fear! This time, too, you have a son." 18With her last breath—for she was at the point of death—she called him Ben-oni; his father, however, named him Benjamin. 19Thus Rachel died; and she was buried on the road to Ephrath [that is, Bethlehem]. 20Jacob set up a memorial stone on her grave, and the same monument marks Rachel's grave to this day.

Jacob continues his journey home. When he meets Esau he is afraid of his anger. But Esau is peaceful; the whole family survives.

While they are still on the journey Rachel goes into labor. She gives birth to a second son, but the childbirth has been too much for her. She dies and is buried on the road to Ephrath, which is interpreted as Bethlehem (cf. also Gen 48:7). There are two traditional sites for the tomb of Rachel, one just outside Bethlehem as this text indicates, and the other at Ramah, five or six miles north of Jerusalem (cf. 1 Sam 10:2; Jer 31:15). There is still a tomb of Rachel near Bethlehem.

Rachel names her son Ben-oni. Jacob names him Benjamin. What do these two names mean? The Hebrew word *'ôn* means "strength," frequently the power of fertility (cf. Gen 49:3; Deut 21:17; Job 40:16; Pss 78:51; 105:36).6 Rachel had earlier asked for another son (Gen 30:24). She names this second son "the son of my strength." Jacob confirms the name by calling the

---

6Sometimes this word is considered to be *'awen*, "trouble" or "sorrow" (cf. Ps 90:10; Hos 9:4). The Greek Septuagint interprets the name *ben-ôni* as "son of my grief."

child *ben-yamin,* "son of my right hand." Or should we inter-
pret Jacob's naming to mean that Rachel is his right hand?

THE MEMORY OF LEAH AND RACHEL

There are a few other significant texts in which Rachel
and/or Leah are mentioned. In his farewell discourse Jacob
says that he buried Leah in Hebron, in the cave where
Abraham and Sarah, Isaac and Rebekah are buried. Jacob
wishes to be buried there with her (Gen 49:28-32). The unloved wife lies with the husband in death. The descendants
of the unloved wife also become more powerful than those of
the beloved wife. Leah's son Judah is the ancestor of David
(1 Sam 17:12; Sir 45:25) and thus of Jesus (Matt 1:3-6; Luke
3:31-33).

Rachel's descendants, the Rachel tribes of Benjamin and of
Joseph's sons Ephraim and Manasseh, do not survive through
the centuries of Israel's history. The tribe of Benjamin is absorbed into Judah. Ephraim and Manasseh (along with Dan
and Naphtali, Rachel tribes through Bilhah) are taken captive
by the Assyrians in the eighth century and do not return.
Jeremiah, reporting the Assyrian captivity, describes the sorrow of Rachel:

> Thus says the LORD:
> In Ramah is heard the sound of moaning,
>   of bitter weeping!
> Rachel mourns her children,
>   she refuses to be consoled
>   because her children are no more (Jer 31:15).

Matthew borrows the text to tell the story of Herod's attempt
to kill the infant Jesus by slaughtering the baby boys of
Bethlehem (Matt 2:18).[7]

The sisters together become a blessing for future mothers
in Israel. When Ruth marries Boaz, the people say, "May the

---

[7]Note that the Jeremiah text is based on the tradition that Rachel was
buried in Ramah and the Matthew text on the tradition that she was
buried near Bethlehem.

L ORD make this wife come into your house like Rachel and Leah, who between them built up the house of Israel. May you do well in Ephrathah and win fame in Bethlehem" (Ruth 4:11). Ruth becomes the mother of Obed, the grandfather of David.

WHO ARE LEAH AND RACHEL?

The two sisters, Rachel and Leah, wives of Jacob, have a complicated story. Their lives are marked by tragedy: Leah is unloved, Rachel is barren and then dies in childbirth. They are set in opposition to one another, and yet there are evidences of cooperation between them. They are the mothers of Israel, the biological mothers of eight of the tribal ancestors and the adoptive mothers of the other four. Jacob favors Rachel's children, Joseph and Benjamin, but in the long view of history it is Leah's son, Judah, who will prevail. Two sisters—both necessary for the story, both major influences on the history of Israel.

THE MAIDS

DEBORAH, REBEKAH'S NURSE

Genesis 24:59; 35:8

At this they allowed their sister Rebekah and her nurse to take leave, along with Abraham's servant and his men.

Death came to Rebekah's nurse Deborah; she was buried under the oak below Bethel, and so it was called Allonbacuth.

Rebekah's nurse is mentioned only twice. When Rebekah leaves her family house, her nurse goes with her. She must have been a young woman when they left Haran.[8] She, too, is

---

[8]Rebekah was married to Isaac twenty years before the twins were born (Gen 25:20, 26). They grow up and Jacob spends twenty years with Laban (Gen 31:38, 41). At the time of her death the nurse has been in service to Rebekah for at least sixty-five to seventy years.

uprooted from her native place, her only security being her relationship with her mistress Rebekah.

The notice of her death raises several questions. Why does it seem that she is returning from Haran with Jacob at the time of her death? Did Rebekah send Deborah to Jacob? Was she sent to help his wives with their children? Did Isaac send her home when Rebekah died? Is this a different woman? Is the verse misplaced?

It is also noteworthy that the tree beneath which she is buried is named Allon-bacuth, "the oak of weeping." Does the name of the tree recall the grief at the death of this faithful old woman? Does the weeping indicate how much she was loved by the children and grandchildren of her mistress? Does she give both her name and her tree to another Deborah, judge of Israel (Judg 4:4-5)?

BILHAH AND ZILPAH

Genesis 29:24, 29

> Laban assigned his slave girl Zilpah to his daughter Leah as her maidservant. . . . Laban assigned his slave girl Bilhah to his daughter Rachel as her maidservant.

The two maidservants of Rachel and Leah, Zilpah and Bilhah, are assigned to their mistresses at the time of their marriage. The announcement is made in identical language. The two women are barely distinguished; they are given no personality. Bilhah and Zilpah are given to Jacob as surrogate mothers by Rachel and Leah (Gen 30:3-12) just as Hagar was given to Abraham by Sarah. The transaction here, however, seems more successful. The sons of Bilhah and Zilpah are adopted by Rachel and Leah and are regarded as members of the family in contrast to the treatment of Ishmael by Sarah. The two maidservants are regularly listed in the genealogies along with their sons (Gen 35:25-26; 46:18, 25). They are the biological mothers of four of the tribes of Israel: Dan and Naphtali, Gad and Asher.

The status of Bilhah and Zilpah, however, is never forgotten. When Jacob meets Esau, he puts the two maidservants and their children in front (Gen 33:1-2). If Esau should attack, these women and their children who are least valued by Jacob will absorb the blow and perhaps protect Leah and Rachel.[9] Bilhah suffers one further tragedy. When Jacob was returning to Canaan, "Reuben went and lay with Bilhah, his father's concubine" (Gen 35:22). Jacob is offended and diminishes Reuben's blessing (Gen 49:3-4), but there is no word of concern for Bilhah, the powerless maidservant.

Two women—servants and pawns in the struggle for sons, nameless, powerless, insignificant, yet mothers of one-third of the tribes of Israel.

DINAH

RAPE AND MASSACRE

Genesis 34:1-7, 24-31

[1]Dinah, the daughter whom Leah had borne to Jacob, went out to visit some of the women of the land. [2]When Shechem, son of Hamor the Hivite, who was chief of the region, saw her, he seized her and lay with her by force. [3]Since he was strongly attracted to Dinah, daughter of Jacob, indeed was really in love with the girl, he endeavored to win her affection. [4]Shechem also asked his father Hamor, "Get me this girl for a wife."

[5]Meanwhile, Jacob heard that Shechem had defiled his daughter Dinah; but since his sons were out in the fields with his livestock, he held his peace until they came home. [6]Now Hamor, the father of Shechem, went out to discuss the matter with Jacob, [7]just as Jacob's sons were coming in from the fields. When they heard the news, the men were shocked and seethed with indignation. What Shechem had done was an outrage in Israel; such a thing could not be tolerated.

[24]All the able-bodied men of the town agreed with Hamor and his son Shechem, and all the males, including every able-bodied man in the community, were circumcised. [25]On the third day, while they were still in pain, Dinah's full brothers Simeon and Levi, two of Jacob's sons, took their swords, advanced against the city without any trouble, and massacred all the males. [26]After they had put Hamor and his

---

[9]Their insignificance is also indicated by the fact that they have become nameless (cf. Gen 32:23).

son Shechem to the sword, they took Dinah from Shechem's house and left. ²⁷Then the other sons of Jacob followed up the slaughter and sacked the city in reprisal for their sister Dinah's defilement. ²⁸They seized their flocks, herds and asses, whatever was in the city and in the country around. ²⁹They carried off all their wealth, their women, and their children, and took for loot whatever was in the houses.

³⁰Jacob said to Simeon and Levi: "You have brought trouble upon me by making me loathsome to the inhabitants of the land, the Canaanites and the Perizzites. I have so few men that, if these people unite against me and attack me, I and my family will be wiped out." ³¹But they retorted, "Should our sister have been treated like a harlot?"

Dinah is the daughter of Leah and Jacob (Gen 30:21; cf. 46:15). She is the only daughter of Jacob named. She is mentioned no doubt because of the story in Genesis 34.

Dinah's story is a story of rape and vengeance. It is a story of men's power and passion. The feelings of Dinah are never described. She suffers the violence of rape. Shechem,[10] who is reported to be "really in love" with her, then wants to marry her (34:3, 8, 11-12, 19). Is she revolted by the thought of marriage to this violent man? Was she in love with him before the rape? Does she feel betrayed? Why is she staying in Shechem's house (cf. 34:26)? Is she imprisoned or is it her choice? We are told nothing.

Dinah's full brothers, Simeon and Levi, are outraged. First they deceive the men of Shechem; then they slaughter them. They do all this because their sister Dinah has been "defiled" (34:5, 13). After the massacre they take Dinah from Shechem's house and leave. Then the rest of Jacob's sons pillage the city "in reprisal for their sister Dinah's defilement" (34:27). Jacob is not happy about their actions, but they reply, "Should our sister have been treated like a harlot?" (34:31).

Dinah has been friendly with the women of the place (34:1). Does the slaughter of the city and the capture of the women and children grieve her? Her brothers now regard her as "defiled" and the incident has marked her with the word

---

[10]The name of Hamor's son, Shechem, is also the name of the place.

"harlot." Will she ever have honor in the family again? Will she ever be allowed to marry? Dinah's fate is not the concern of the chapter. The narrator is more interested in the defeat of Shechem by Simeon and Levi. Dinah is condemned to oblivion.

TAMAR

A Righteous Woman

Genesis 38:6-30

⁶Judah got a wife named Tamar for his first-born, Er. ⁷But Er, Judah's first-born, greatly offended the LORD; so the LORD took his life. ⁸Then Judah said to Onan, "Unite with your brother's widow, in fulfillment of your duty as brother-in-law, and thus preserve your brother's line." ⁹Onan, however, knew that the descendants would not be counted as his; so whenever he had relations with his brother's widow, he wasted his seed on the ground, to avoid contributing off-spring for his brother. ¹⁰What he did greatly offended the LORD, and the LORD took his life too. ¹¹Thereupon Judah said to his daughter-in-law Tamar, "Stay as a widow in your father's house until my son Shelah grows up"—for he feared that Shelah also might die like his brothers. So Tamar went to live in her father's house.

¹²Years passed, and Judah's wife, the daughter of Shua, died. After Judah completed the period of mourning, he went up to Timnah for the shearing of his sheep, in company with his friend Hirah the Adullamite. ¹³When Tamar was told that her father-in-law was on his way up to Timnah to shear his sheep, ¹⁴she took off her widow's garb, veiled her face by covering herself with a shawl, and sat down at the entrance to Enaim, which is on the way to Timnah; for she was aware that, although Shelah was now grown up, she had not been given to him in marriage. ¹⁵When Judah saw her, he mistook her for a harlot, since she had covered her face. ¹⁶So he went over to her at the roadside, and not realizing that she was his daughter-in-law, he said, "Come, let me have intercourse with you." She replied, "What will you pay me for letting you have intercourse with me?" ¹⁷He answered, "I will send you a kid from the flock." "Very well," she said, "provided you leave a pledge until you send it." ¹⁸Judah asked, "What pledge am I to give to you?" She answered, "Your seal and cord, and the staff you carry." So

he gave them to her and had intercourse with her, and she conceived by him. [19]When she went away, she took off her shawl and put on her widow's garb again.

[20]Judah sent the kid by his friend the Adullamite to recover the pledge from the woman; but he could not find her. [21]So he asked the men of the place, "Where is the temple prostitute, the one by the roadside in Enaim?" But they answered, "There has never been a temple prostitute here." [22]He went back to Judah and told him, "I could not find her; and besides, the men of the place said there was no temple prostitute there." [23]"Let her keep the things," Judah replied; "otherwise we shall become a laughingstock. After all, I did send her the kid, even though you were unable to find her."

[24]About three months later, Judah was told that his daughter-in-law Tamar had played the harlot and was then with child from her harlotry. "Bring her out," cried Judah; "she shall be burned." [25]But as they were bringing her out, she sent word to her father-in-law, "It is by the man to whom these things belong that I am with child. Please verify," she added, "whose seal and cord and whose staff these are." [26]Judah recognized them and said, "She is more in the right than I am, since I did not give her to my son Shelah." But he had no further relations with her.

[27]When the time of her delivery came, she was found to have twins in her womb. [28]While she was giving birth, one infant put out his hand; and the midwife, taking a crimson thread, tied it on his hand, to note that this one came out first. [29]But as he withdrew his hand, his brother came out; and she said, "What a breach you have made for yourself!" So he was called Perez. [30]Afterward his brother came out; he was called Zerah.

The story of Tamar is the story of another woman who uses unorthodox means in order to ensure the succession of descendants. Tamar, probably a Canaanite, is given in marriage to Judah's son Er. When Er dies because of his sinfulness, she is given to his brother Onan.[11] Onan does not want to honor the obligation to his dead brother, so God takes his life also.

---

[11]The practice of giving a widow to the surviving brother-in-law is called levirate marriage from the Latin word for brother-in-law, *levir*. The

Tamar is now doubly widowed. Judah has a third son, but is afraid that marriage with Tamar will be deadly for this son also. So Tamar is instructed to return to her father's house and wait. Tamar, however, is not free. She is promised to the third son, Shelah, and must marry him or no one.

Tamar waits for years. Judah apparently has no intention of honoring the obligation to his dead son Er. So Tamar takes matters into her own hands. She disguises herself and waits for Judah on the way to Timnah. Judah mistakes her for a harlot, contracts with her, and has intercourse with her. Each of these statements is significant.

Judah mistakes her for a harlot or temple prostitute. He sends the fee the next day, but the people of the place say, "There has never been a temple prostitute here." Later Tamar is accused of "playing the harlot." Nowhere does the text claim that she *is* a harlot. The people in the story, however, mistake her for one.

Tamar contracts with Judah: intercourse for a fee. She is not interested in payment, however; she is interested in identification. She asks for Judah's seal, cord, and staff. She is not available for the payment of the fee, so she keeps the pledge. These items will save her life when she is about to be executed for adultery.

Judah has intercourse with Tamar and she conceives. In the midst of the stories of barren women, Tamar conceives immediately. She gives birth to twins, Perez and Zerah. She herself has provided descendants for her dead husband and continued the line of Judah.

Judah's response to the discovery that he is the man responsible for Tamar's pregnancy, a situation for which he is about to execute her, is the key to the story. Judah exclaims,

---

purpose is to provide descendants for the dead man. In a society such as ancient Israel, in which there is no belief in real life after death, children are the only way a person continues to exist. There are also two subordinate purposes: the property of the dead man remains within the tribe and clan; the widow is taken care of. There was some resistance to the practice for economic reasons: raising up children for the dead man would diminish the inheritance of the brother-in-law's children. The arrival of a second wife may have also introduced tension into the household.

"She is more righteous than I am" (38:26). Righteousness in the Bible is always based on relationship. Tamar has honored the demands of the relationship with her dead husband whereas Judah has not. Thus Tamar is more righteous than Judah. She has taken on the responsibility of another and been judged guilty because of it. She has taken unconventional risks, broken the accepted pattern, and been judged guilty because of it. Yet in the end she is judged to be more righteous than the other main character in the story because she has honored the demands of the relationship.

Tamar's son Perez is an ancestor of David. Generations later, Boaz, husband of Ruth, will be blessed in her name: "With the offspring the LORD will give you from this girl, may your house become like the house of Perez, whom Tamar bore to Judah" (Ruth 4:12). Tamar is thus an ancestor of Jesus, son of David of the tribe of Judah. She herself is mentioned in the genealogy of Jesus in Matthew (Matt 1:3). She is one of Jesus' great-grandmothers.

3. Women of Israel's Passover

Suggested readings: Exodus 1–2; 4:19-26; 15:1-21; 18:1-7; Numbers 12:1-16; 20:1; 27:1-11; 36:1-13; Joshua 17:1-6; Micah 6:4.

The beginning of the story of Israel's deliverance is a story of heroic women: the midwives, Moses' mother and sister, Pharaoh's daughter and her maids. With the help of these courageous women, the oppression of the Egyptians was broken.

THE MIDWIVES: SHIPHRAH AND PUAH

Exodus 1:15-22

15The king of Egypt told the Hebrew midwives, one of whom was called Shiphrah and the other Puah, 16"When you act as midwives for the Hebrew women and see them giving birth, if it is a boy, kill him; but if it is a girl, she may live." 17The midwives, however, feared God; they did not do as the king of Egypt had ordered them, but let the boys live. 18So the king summoned the midwives and asked them, "Why have you acted thus, allowing the boys to live?" 19The midwives answered Pharaoh, "The Hebrew women are not like the Egyptian women. They are robust and give birth before the midwife arrives." 20Therefore God dealt well with the midwives. The people, too, increased and grew strong. 21And because the midwives feared God, he built up families for them. 22Pharaoh then commanded all his subjects, "Throw into the river every boy that is born to the Hebrews, but you may let all the girls live."

The story of the midwives interrupts the story of Israel's forced labor in Egypt. The oppressors move from slavery to genocide. The agents in this atrocity are to be the midwives. At the moment of birth they are to kill each male baby.

Two midwives are singled out to represent the many required to serve Israel's growing population. The two are given names, surprising in this story in which many women remain nameless. The name of one is Shiphrah, "fair one," and the other is Puah, probably meaning "girl." It is possible that the women are Egyptian; the phrase in 1:15 can be translated "midwives to the Hebrews." This gives greater credibility to Pharaoh's expectation that they will obey his command.

Shiphrah and Puah, however, resist Pharaoh's order. They do not kill Hebrew baby boys. When they are summoned before the Pharaoh they make a lame excuse: "The Hebrew women are stronger than Egyptian women. They give birth before we arrive." The story continues to be surprising. They get away with their civil disobedience and their limp explanation. These women illustrate the principle that the only way to break oppression is to refuse to be oppressed. Pharaoh gives up on the women as agents of genocide; instead he commands all his people to kill Hebrew baby boys.

The Hebrew text claims that the women acted so bravely because they feared God. Fear of the Lord is awe and reverence in the recognition of the power and goodness of God. It is wonder in the face of God's overwhelming love. It is trust in the wisdom of God who is more than we can ever imagine. Fear of the Lord is the beginning of wisdom (cf. Ps 111:10; Prov 9:11) and the distinguishing characteristic of those who are faithful to God's covenant (cf. Deut 6:1-3; Pss 25:14; 34:10).

Because the midwives stand in this right relationship to the living God, they have the courage to honor God's commands. Their reward is the gift of life. God builds up families for them. The implication is that they become part of the covenant people of Israel. They become channels of life for the covenant people. They are the midwives assisting at the birth of Israel.

MOSES' MOTHER

Exodus 2:1-10

1Now a certain man of the house of Levi married a Levite woman, 2who conceived and bore a son. Seeing that he was a goodly child, she hid him for three months. [3]When she could hide him no longer, she took a papyrus basket, daubed it with bitumen and pitch, and putting the child in it, placed it among the reeds on the river bank. [4]His sister stationed herself at a distance to find out what would happen to him.

[5]Pharaoh's daughter came down to the river to bathe, while her maids walked along the river bank. Noticing the basket among the reeds, she sent her handmaid to fetch it. [6]On opening it, she looked, and lo, there was a baby boy, crying! She was moved with pity for him and said, "It is one of the Hebrews' children." [7]Then his sister asked Pharaoh's daughter, "Shall I go and call one of the Hebrew women to nurse the child for you?" [8]"Yes, do so," she answered. So the maiden went and called the child's own mother. [9]Pharaoh's daughter said to her, "Take this child and nurse it for me, and I will repay you." The woman therefore took the child and nursed it. [10]When the child grew, she brought him to Pharaoh's daughter, who adopted him as her son and called him Moses; for she said, "I drew him out of the water."

Moses' mother gives birth to the hero of Israel's deliverance and continues the story of resistance to oppression. Although she is nameless in this account,[1] she is described in terms that suggest major figures in the rest of Israel's history. After she gives birth she looks at the child and sees *how good (kî tôb)* he is. Just so God looks at the various elements of creation brought forth and says, "How good *(kî tôb)!*" (Gen 1:4, 10, 12, 18, 21, 25). She saves the child from the river by means of a vessel (literally an "ark," *tebah*) daubed with bitumen and pitch. Just so Noah saved human and animal life from the flood by means of an ark *(tebah)* covered with pitch (Gen 6:14). She endangers the child, turning him over to strangers, and then receives him back with payment (Exod 2:9). Just so Abraham endangered Sarah and then received her back with added riches (Gen 20:1-18). This mother is described as a source of life for Israel like Noah and Abraham, even like God.

[1]Moses' mother is named Jochebed in Exod 6:16-20 and Num 26:58-59. These passages come from the later Priestly tradition that commonly gave names to previously unnamed figures who were significant for Israel's story.

PHARAOH'S DAUGHTER

Pharaoh's daughter is another of the courageous women who are found at the beginning of the Exodus story. The story is simple; the questions are many. This daughter of the man who has commanded that all Hebrew baby boys be thrown into the river sees a baby boy in the river and pities him. She knows the child is Hebrew; she knows why he is in the river. Still she gives the child to a Hebrew woman to nurse and then adopts him as her son. She acts in defiance of her father's order, but her defiance is subtle. She does not confront her father with his injustice. She simply reverses his command. Her action, like that of the midwives, renders the Pharaoh powerless. The way to break oppression is to refuse to be oppressed.

Pharaoh's daughter gives the Hebrew baby an Egyptian name, Moses.[2] She raises him in the Egyptian court. She prepares him for the task God has in mind for him. She trains Moses in the skills which will enable him to confront and eventually defeat another Pharaoh. She is a mother of the exodus.

The biblical text reveals no more. We do not know her name, her motivations, or what happens to her after this scene.

MIRIAM

SISTER OF MOSES

Exodus 2:7-8

7Then his sister asked Pharaoh's daughter, "Shall I go and call one of the Hebrew women to nurse the child for you?" 8"Yes, do so," she answered. So the maiden went and called the child's own mother.

The notice in Exod 2:7 that the baby Moses has an older sister comes as a surprise. The first verses of this chapter suggest

---

[2]The name "Moses" means "to be born." It is found in the names of Thut*mose*, Ah*mose*, and Ra*meses*. Later biblical tradition will give the name a Hebrew etymology from the Hebrew word, "to draw out."

that Moses is the first child of the Levite man and woman. In Exodus 2 the baby's sister is regarded as doubly insignificant: her birth is not mentioned; her name is not given. Yet she, along with the women discussed previously, is a major actor in this scene of deliverance. She is the liaison between Pharaoh's daughter and Moses' mother. This young girl links the women of Egypt and the women of Israel in the act of saving Moses. She has waited bravely, guarding the child; now her action restores the child to his mother.

A sister of Moses is named in the genealogies: Miriam (cf. Exod 6:20; Num 26:59; 1 Chron 5:29).[3] The meaning of her name is not certain. Like the name of Moses, it is probably an Egyptian name meaning "beloved." The Greek form of the name appears frequently in the New Testament, most notably of Mary, the mother of Jesus, Mary of Bethany, and Mary Magdalene. The genealogies list the three major leaders of the exodus-wilderness period—Aaron, Moses, and Miriam—as children of one family.

PROPHET OF VICTORY

Exodus 15:20-21

> [20]The prophetess Miriam, Aaron's sister, took a tambourine in her hand, while all the women went out after her with tambourines, dancing; [21]and she led them in the refrain:
>
> > Sing to the LORD, for he is gloriously triumphant;
> > horse and chariot he has cast into the sea.

The song of Miriam at the crossing of the sea is one of the oldest texts in the Bible. Miriam leads the community in the cultic celebration of victory, setting a precedent for the Holy War tradition. Two centuries later the daughter of Jephthah will come out dancing with tambourines to meet her father after his victory over the Ammonites (Judg 11:34). The heroine Judith will lead the celebration after the defeat of the Assyrians: the women dancing, the men singing hymns (Jdt 15:12–16:2). In the Holy War tradition the victory is due to God's gift, not human power (cf. Judg 7:1-7; Ps 20:8). The

---

[3]It is not certain that the nameless sister in Exodus 2 is Miriam.

battle is seen as part of a liturgical celebration (see the fall of Jericho in Joshua 6); the victory song led by the women is the conclusion to the liturgy. Miriam is the first to lead such a song; she celebrates God's victory over slavery and death.

Miriam is identified as a prophet. The function of a prophet is to be a messenger for God. The prophet has a ministry of imagination, leading the people to understand their present experience and to imagine—and thus be able to achieve—a better future. Miriam's song interprets the exodus experience for the people as God's gift of new life. This gift of new life reveals God's power used in their behalf (Exod 15:2-10). Miriam's song also describes their glorious new future in the land of promise (Exod 15:11-18).

CHALLENGE TO MOSES

Numbers 12:1-16

¹While they were in Hazeroth, Miriam and Aaron spoke against Moses on the pretext of the marriage he had contracted with a Cushite woman. ²They complained, "Is it through Moses alone that the LORD speaks? Does he not speak through us also?" And the LORD heard this. ³Now, Moses himself was by far the meekest man on the face of the earth. ⁴So at once the LORD said to Moses and Aaron and Miriam, "Come out, you three, to the meeting tent." And the three of them went. ⁵Then the LORD came down in the column of cloud, and standing at the entrance of the tent, called Aaron and Miriam. When both came forward, ⁶he said, "Now listen to the words of the LORD:

Should there be a prophet among you,
    in visions will I reveal myself to him,
    in dreams will I speak to him;
7 Not so with my servant Moses!
    Throughout my house he bears my trust:
8   face to face I speak to him,
        plainly and not in riddles.
    The presence of the LORD he beholds.

Why, then, did you not fear to speak against my servant Moses?"

⁹So angry was the LORD against them that when he departed, ¹⁰and the cloud withdrew from the tent, there was

Miriam, a snow-white leper! When Aaron turned and saw her a leper, [11]"Ah, my lord!" he said to Moses, "please do not charge us with the sin that we have foolishly committed! [12]Let her not thus be like the stillborn babe that comes forth from its mother's womb with its flesh half consumed." [13]Then Moses cried to the LORD, "Please, not this! Pray, heal her!" [14]But the LORD answered Moses, "Suppose her father had spit in her face, would she not hide in shame for seven days? Let her be confined outside the camp for seven days; only then may she be brought back." [15]So Miriam was confined outside the camp for seven days, and the people did not start out again until she was brought back.

[16]After that the people set out from Hazeroth and encamped in the desert of Paran.

The question of Miriam's role arises in Numbers 12. She challenges the religious leadership of Moses. Miriam, Aaron, and Moses are certainly the major leaders of the exodus-wilderness period. Is one among them primary? "Is it through Moses alone that the LORD speaks?" (12:2). Prophetic authority is the real question. Moses' foreign wife is a secondary matter.

God's answer to the question is clear and swift. God may speak through Miriam and Aaron as through other prophets, but Moses is the primary witness. God speaks to him face to face. Any challenges to his leadership, religious or civil, are terribly punished (cf. Num 16:1–17:15). Miriam is struck immediately with a skin disease. Her condition wrings a plea from Aaron and a prayer from Moses. But any skin disease, however temporary, requires that the sufferer be confined outside the camp (cf. Lev 13:4-6). Miriam is separated from the community, but the community will not leave without her. They wait for her restoration before continuing their journey.

Miriam's suffering is remembered in the deuteronomic legislation concerning leprosy (Deut 24:8-9).

DEATH OF MIRIAM

Numbers 20:1

[1]The whole Israelite community arrived in the desert of Zin in the first month, and the people settled at Kadesh. It was here that Miriam died, and here that she was buried.

Numbers 20 indicates that the three desert leaders die in the desert. Miriam's death is reported at the beginning of the chapter, Aaron's death at the end (20:22-29). In between God tells Moses that he will die before the entrance to the land of promise (20:12). Miriam, Moses, and Aaron led Israel out of Egypt and through the desert. It will be the task of the next generation to enter the land.

Miriam is buried at Kadesh, an important sanctuary on Israel's route through the desert. The very name of the place means "sacred." The Israelites encamp there for a long time (cf. Deut 1:46). There the spies make their report on the land (Num 13:25-33); there the people murmur and are told that they will wander in the desert for forty years (Numbers 14). From there the final journey into the land begins (Num 20:14-22). The notice of Miriam's burial associates her clearly with this significant sanctuary of the desert period.

A LASTING MEMORY

Micah 6:3-4

3O my people, what have I done to you,
   or how have I wearied you? Answer me!
4For I brought you up from the land of Egypt,
   from the place of slavery I released you;
And I sent before you Moses,
   Aaron, and Miriam.

The memory of Miriam continues through the prophetic period. In the eighth century the prophet Micah lists her as one of the great desert leaders, along with Moses and Aaron. She is part of God's gift to the people in the great saving event of the exodus. Micah reports a lawsuit in which God accuses the people of forgetting these wonderful deeds. The people plead guilty and suggest various means of making amends. But God is not satisfied with their offers. God's sentence is more difficult. God demands, not that they remove something from their lives, but that they live fully: "to do the right and to love goodness, and to walk humbly with your God" (Mic 6:8).

Who is Miriam? Some things are certain: She is one of the three great heroes in the desert, equal to Aaron and Moses. She is a cultic leader and prophet, celebrating the divine victory at the sea and mediating God's word to the people. She is respected by the people. They remain at Hazeroth during the seven days of her isolation; their journey will not continue until Miriam is with them. Her story is attached to the sanctuary of Kadesh, a significant site in Israel's desert sojourn.

The image associated with Miriam is water. As the nameless sister in Exodus 2, she watches the baby in the river. She sings the victory song after the crossing of the sea. She dies at Kadesh where the people complain because they have no water (Num 20:2-5). Her story is as paradoxical as the image of water which is a symbol of both life and death.

MOSES' WIFE: ZIPPORAH

BETROTHAL AND MARRIAGE

Exodus 2:15-22

> But Moses fled from him and stayed in the land of Midian. As he was seated there by a well, 16seven daughters of a priest of Midian came to draw water and fill the troughs to water their father's flock. 17But some shepherds came and drove them away. Then Moses got up and defended them and watered their flock. 18When they returned to their father Reuel, he said to them, "How is it you have returned so soon today?" 19They answered, "An Egyptian saved us from the interference of the shepherds. He even drew water for us and watered the flock!" 20"Where is the man?" he asked his daughters. "Why did you leave him there? Invite him to have something to eat." 21Moses agreed to live with him, and the man gave him his daughter Zipporah in marriage. 22She bore him a son, whom he named Gershom; for he said, "I am a stranger in a foreign land."

The story of Moses' betrothal to Zipporah is another betrothal type scene (cf. Genesis 24). Several of the elements of the typical scene are found: a stranger, a well, young women, the drawing of water, an invitation to a meal. One element of the type scene is heightened in this story. Instead of one young woman, there are seven. The number seven often indicates completeness or perfection. Moses is met by a perfect number of young women. He chooses one from this perfection to be his wife. The use of the type scene puts the marriage of Moses and Zipporah in the tradition of the ancestors.

Zipporah, whose name means "swallow," is identified as a daughter of Reuel, a priest of Midian. Moses' genealogy has put him in the family of Levi, a priestly family; his wife also belongs to a priestly family.

Zipporah does not belong to the tradition of barren wives. She bears Moses a son whom Moses names Gershom. The name of the son, from the Hebrew word *ger* which means "sojourner," signifies that Moses is not a permanent resident of Midian. Zipporah's son is the sign of Moses' future return to his people.

SAVIOR OF MOSES

Exodus 4:19-20, 24-26

> 19In Midian the LORD said to Moses, "Go back to Egypt, for all the men who sought your life are dead." 20So Moses took his wife and his sons, and started back to the land of Egypt, with them riding the ass. The staff of God he carried with him.

> 24On the journey, at a place where they spent the night, the LORD came upon Moses and would have killed him. 25But Zipporah took a piece of flint and cut off her son's foreskin and, touching his person, she said, "You are a spouse of blood to me." 26Then God let Moses go. At that time she said, "A spouse of blood," in regard to the circumcision.

The scene in which God would kill Moses is puzzling. It is similar to Gen 32:23-31 when God wrestles with Jacob. Both scenes portray God as dangerous and terrifying. God is a night spirit threatening the chosen one as he returns home. In the Genesis story, Jacob holds his own against God and thus wins the name Israel, "the one who wrestles with God." Moses, on the other hand, is saved by his wife Zipporah. She is the sixth woman in the story of Moses who functions prominently in saving lives: the midwives who save the Israelite baby boys, the mother and sister of Moses, and Pharaoh's daughter, each of whom saves Moses' life.

The act of saving is a circumcision. The story shows Zipporah circumcising her son and touching Moses' penis with the bloody foreskin. It is frequently supposed, however, that this story is a veiling of the true event of Zipporah circumcising her husband Moses. In either case Zipporah saves Moses' life, circumcising him physically or symbolically by touching his penis with the blood of their son's circumcision.

There are several reasons why it is imperative that Moses be circumcised. Circumcision is the sign of God's covenant with Abraham and his descendants (Gen 17:10-14). If Moses is not circumcised, he is cut off from God's people (cf. Gen 17:14). Moses, who is called to save the covenant people, must bear the sign of the covenant in his flesh. Circumcision is also a qualification for participating in the Passover celebration, a memorial of Israel's deliverance from Egypt. Moses, who is God's instrument in the deliverance, must himself be circumcised. Finally, although Israel circumcised baby boys on the eighth day after birth (Lev 12:3), circumcision seems originally to have been practiced in the Ancient Near East as a rite of initiation, either from boyhood into manhood (cf. the circumcision of Ishmael at the age of thirteen, Gen 17:25) or as a preparation for marriage. When Zipporah touches Moses with the bloody foreskin, she says, "You are a spouse of blood to me."

Zipporah's action is unique and redemptive. Ordinarily circumcision is performed by the father; there is no other biblical story of a woman circumcising anyone. By her action, Zipporah saves Moses' life. She delivers Moses from death, as Moses will deliver the Israelites. She stands between Moses and an angry God. God gives her the moment and she becomes a mediator, just as Moses does when God threatens to destroy the people because of the golden calf (Exod 32:1-14).

A WORTHY WIFE

Zipporah is a significant figure in the life of Israel's great hero, Moses. She becomes his wife in the tradition of Sarah, Rebekah, and Rachel. She saves his life in a dangerous encounter with God and initiates him into the covenant. She bears him two sons whose names tell the story of Moses' career: Gershom, "I am a stranger in a strange land"; and Eliezer, "my father's God is my helper; he has rescued me from Pharaoh's sword." Zipporah is a wife worthy of Moses.

4. Women of Israel's Early Tribes

Suggested Readings: Joshua 2:1-24; 6:20-25; Judges 4:1–5:31; 11:1–40; 13:1–16:31.

RAHAB

THE HARLOT

Joshua 2:1-21

¹Then Joshua, son of Nun, secretly sent out two spies from Shittim, saying, "Go, reconnoiter the land and Jericho." When the two reached Jericho, they went into the house of a harlot named Rahab, where they lodged. ²But a report was brought to the king of Jericho that some Israelites had come there that night to spy out the land. ³So the king of Jericho sent Rahab the order, "Put out the visitors who have entered your house, for they have come to spy out the entire land." ⁴The woman had taken the two men and hidden them, so she said, "True, the men you speak of came to me, but I did not know where they came from. ⁵At dark, when it was time for the gate to be shut, they left, and I do not know where they went. You will have to pursue them immediately to overtake them." ⁶Now, she had led them to the roof, and hidden them among her stalks of flax spread out there. ⁷But the pursuers set out along the way to the fords of the Jordan, and once they had left, the gate was shut.

⁸Before the spies fell asleep, Rahab came to them on the roof ⁹and said: "I know that the LORD has given you the land, that a dread of you has come upon us, and that all the inhabitants of the land are overcome with fear of you. ¹⁰For we have heard how the LORD dried up the waters of the Red Sea before you when you came out of Egypt, and how you dealt with Sihon and Og, the two kings of the Amorites beyond the Jordan, whom you doomed to destruction. ¹¹At these reports, we are disheartened; everyone is discouraged because of you,

since the LORD, your God, is God in heaven above and on earth below. [12]Now then, swear to me by the LORD that, since I am showing kindness to you, you in turn will show kindness to my family; and give me an unmistakable token [13]that you are to spare my father and mother, brothers and sisters, and all their kin, and save us from death." [14]"We pledge our lives for yours," the men answered her. "If you do not betray this errand of ours, we will be faithful in showing kindness to you when the LORD gives us the land."

[15]Then she let them down through the window with a rope; for she lived in a house built into the city wall. [16]"Go up into the hill country," she suggested to them, "that your pursuers may not find you. Hide there for three days, until they return; then you may proceed on your way." [17]The men answered her, "This is how we will fulfill the oath you made us take: [18]When we come into the land, tie this scarlet cord in the window through which you are letting us down; and gather your father and mother, your brothers and all your family into your house. [19]Should any of them pass outside the doors of your house, he will be responsible for his own death, and we shall be guiltless. But we shall be responsible if anyone in the house with you is harmed. [20]If, however, you betray this errand of ours, we shall be quit of the oath you have made us take." [21]"Let it be as you say," she replied, and bade them farewell. When they were gone, she tied the scarlet cord in the window.

Just as women were instrumental in the exodus of Israel from Egypt, so a woman is significant in Israel's entrance into the promised land. The spies sent by Joshua to reconnoiter the land stay in the house of a woman named Rahab, who is identified as a harlot. The possibility that her house is a brothel is further suggested by the statement that the spies "lay" there (2:1), a word with strong sexual connotations. Her house, or inn, is built into the city wall. Her family also lives in the city—father, mother, brothers, etc. (6:23). No husband or children are mentioned; she is a working woman, responsible for her own support.

Later tradition modified the image of Rahab. Josephus, a first-century Jewish historian, calls her simply an inn-keeper.[1]

[1]Josephus, *Ant.*, 5.1 §2.

It is not surprising that the two professions of prostitute and inn-keeper are mingled; often prejudice assumes that if a woman keeps a hotel she must be a prostitute or a madam.

News collects at an inn; strangers are less conspicuous there. Perhaps this is why the spies choose to stay with Rahab who herself has heard the news about the Israelites encamped across the Jordan. She not only knows of the exodus and the victories over local kings; she knows that God has given them the land. Her speech (2:9-13) is a testimony of faith in the God of Israel.

Her faith is manifested not only in words, but also in actions. She shows *hesed*, faithful covenant love, to the spies (2:12). She hides them and sends their pursuers on a wild goose chase. Having shown *hesed* to the spies, she requests *hesed* in return. She asks that they spare her family in the battle for Jericho. The men pledge to do so. This Canaanite woman represents the many Canaanites who will join Israel and become part of the covenant people. The repetition of the covenant virtues—*hesed* and *'emeth* (love and fidelity)—signifies Rahab's entrance into the covenant (Josh 2:12-14; cf. 6:25).

IN THE MIDST OF ISRAEL

Joshua 6:20-25

20As the horns blew, the people began to shout. When they heard the signal horn, they raised a tremendous shout. The wall collapsed, and the people stormed the city in a frontal attack and took it. 21They observed the ban by putting to the sword all living creatures in the city: men and women, young and old, as well as oxen, sheep and asses.

22Joshua directed the two men who had spied out the land, "Go into the harlot's house and bring out the woman with all her kin, as you swore to her you would do." 23The spies entered and brought out Rahab, with her father, mother, brothers, and all her kin. Her entire family they led forth and placed them outside the camp of Israel. 24The city itself they burned with all that was in it, except the silver, gold, and articles of bronze and iron, which were placed in the treasury of the house of the LORD. 25Because Rahab the harlot had hidden the messengers whom Joshua had sent to reconnoiter Jericho, Joshua spared her with her family and all her kin, who continue in the midst of Israel to this day.

Jericho is the first city in the land taken by the entering Israelites. In taking the city they carry out the customs of Holy War. One such custom is the *herem*, or ban. There are no prisoners captured; there is no plunder taken. No one is to get rich from war. Therefore all living things are killed, all material things destroyed. It is a harsh custom. There are to be no exceptions.

The threat to Rahab and her family is obvious. The spies, however, are faithful to their word. The command is given to put everything in the city under the ban except Rahab and her family (Josh 6:17). Joshua sends the spies themselves to fetch her and her family.

Rahab is an independent business woman who deceives her king in order to protect Israel. She is a courageous woman who entrusts her future and that of her family to an unknown people and an unknown God. She has heard of this God, however. She already practices covenant virtues and expects them in return. God answers her trust with generous love. She and her family "continue in the midst of Israel to this day," a part of God's covenant people.

She is named in the Letter to the Hebrews as an example of faith: "By faith Rahab the harlot did not perish with the disobedient, for she had received the spies in peace" (Heb 11:31). The Letter of James singles her out along with Abraham as an example of someone who demonstrates faith by good works: ". . . was not Rahab the harlot also justified by works when she welcomed the messengers and sent them out by a different route?" (Jas 2:25). She is one of the five women listed in Matthew's genealogy of Jesus (Matt 1:5). She is named as the mother of Boaz who will marry Ruth, another foreign woman who practices the covenant virtue of *hesed* and becomes a mother in Israel and a great-grandmother of Jesus.

DEBORAH AND JAEL

THE JUDGE

Judges 4:1-16

1After Ehud's death, however, the Israelites again offended the LORD. 2So the LORD allowed them to fall into the power of the Canaanite king, Jabin, who reigned in Hazor. The general of his army was Sisera, who dwelt in Harosheth-ha-goiim. ³But the Israelites cried out to the LORD; for with his nine hundred iron chariots he sorely oppressed the Israelites for twenty years.

⁴At this time the prophetess Deborah, wife of Lappidoth, was judging Israel. ⁵She used to sit under Deborah's palm tree, situated between Ramah and Bethel in the mountain region of Ephraim, and there the Israelites came up to her for judgment. ⁶She sent and summoned Barak, son of Abinoam, from Kedesh of Naphtali. "This is what the LORD, the God of Israel, commands," she said to him; "go, march on Mount Tabor, and take with you ten thousand Naphtalites and Zebulunites. ⁷I will lead Sisera, the general of Jabin's army, out to you at the Wadi Kishon, together with his chariots and troops, and will deliver them into your power." ⁸But Barak answered her, "If you come with me, I will go; if you do not come with me, I will not go." ⁹"I will certainly go with you," she replied, "but you shall not gain the glory in the expedition on which you are setting out, for the LORD will have Sisera fall into the power of a woman." So Deborah joined Barak and journeyed with him to Kedesh.

¹⁰Barak summoned Zebulun and Naphtali to Kedesh, and ten thousand men followed him. Deborah also went up with him. ¹¹Now the Kenite Heber had detached himself from his own people, the descendants of Hobab, Moses' brother-in-law, and had pitched his tent by the terebinth of Zaanannim, which was near Kedesh.

¹²It was reported to Sisera that Barak, son of Abinoam, had gone up to Mount Tabor. ¹³So Sisera assembled from Harosheth-ha-goiim at the Wadi Kishon all nine hundred of his iron chariots and all his forces. ¹⁴Deborah then said to Barak, "Be off, for this is the day on which the LORD has delivered Sisera into your power. The LORD marches before you." So Barak went down Mount Tabor, followed by his ten thousand men. ¹⁵And the LORD put Sisera and all his chariots and all his forces to rout before Barak. Sisera himself dismounted from his chariot and fled on foot. ¹⁶Barak, however, pursued the chariots and the army as far as Harosheth-ha-goiim. The entire army of Sisera fell beneath the sword, not even one man surviving.

The Book of Judges is a collection of hero stories from Israel's frontier period. There are twelve stories, linked by the same pattern: (1) Israel offends God; (2) God is angry and gives (literally, sells) them to their enemies; (3) The Israelites cry out; (4) God sends someone called a judge to save them, and (5) the land has rest for X years. When the judge dies, the pattern repeats.

Deborah is one of the twelve judge-heroes. Most of the judges were military heroes; a few were assassins. In the Book of Judges, only Deborah acts as a "judge" in modern terminology, settling disputes. She is called a prophet, one who speaks the word of God. Her name is Deborah, which means "honey-bee," or "leader." She is called the wife of Lappidoth, which may be translated, "the woman of torches." She sits under Deborah's palm tree and exercises judgment. Is the tree named for her? Or is the tree named for Rebekah's beloved maid, who was buried under the "tree of weeping" (Gen 35:8)?

As the deadly cycle of sin and suffering begins, Deborah summons a man, Barak,[2] to function as the military leader. Although she, a woman, is judge and prophet, she is not likely to succeed in the role of army general. It is she, however, who outlines the strategy for the battle (4:6-7) and determines the moment of attack (4:14). Deborah, the prophet, announces the word of the Lord; Barak, the general, follows her command. Barak is well aware that she holds the power: he refuses to take the commission unless she goes with him. She also is aware of her power: she informs him that the glory of victory will not fall to him but to a woman (4:8-9).

Judges 5:1-23

1On that day Deborah [and Barak, son of Abinoam,] sang this song:

2Of chiefs who took the lead in Israel,
    of noble deeds by the people who bless the Lord,
3Hear, O kings! Give ear, O princes!
    I to the Lord will sing my song,
    my hymn to the Lord, the God of Israel.

2Barak's name means "lightning." He wins the battle in a storm.

4O LORD, when you went out from Seir,
  when you marched from the land of Edom,
The earth quaked and the heavens were shaken,
  while the clouds sent down showers.
5Mountains trembled
  in the presence of the LORD, the One of Sinai,
  in the presence of the LORD, the God of Israel.

6In the days of Shamgar, son of Anath,
  in the days of slavery caravans ceased:
Those who traveled the roads
  went by roundabout paths.
7Gone was freedom beyond the walls,
  gone indeed from Israel.

When I, Deborah, rose,
  when I rose, a mother in Israel,
8New gods were their choice;
  then the war was at their gates.
Not a shield could be seen, nor a lance,
  among forty thousand in Israel!

9My heart is with the leaders of Israel,
  nobles of the people who bless the LORD;
10They who ride on white asses,
  seated on saddlecloths as they go their way;
11Sing of them to the strains of the harpers at the wells,
  where men recount the just deeds of the LORD,
  his just deeds that brought freedom to Israel.

12Awake, awake, Deborah!
  awake, awake, strike up a song.
Strength! arise, Barak,
  make despoilers your spoil, son of Abinoam.
13Then down came the fugitives with the mighty,
  the people of the LORD came down for me as warriors.

14From Ephraim, princes were in the valley;
  behind you was Benjamin, among your troops.
From Machir came down commanders,
  from Zebulun wielders of the marshal's staff.

15With Deborah were the princes of Issachar;
  Barak, too, was in the valley, his course unchecked.

Among the clans of Reuben
  great were the searchings of heart.

16Why do you stay beside your hearths
   listening to the lowing of the herds?
Among the clans of Reuben
   great were the searchings of heart!

17Gilead, beyond the Jordan, rests;
   why does Dan spend his time in ships?
Asher, who dwells along the shore,
   is resting in his coves.
18Zebulun is the people defying death;
   Naphtali, too, on the open heights!

19The kings came and fought;
   then they fought, those kings of Canaan,
At Taanach by the waters of Megiddo;
   no silver booty did they take.
20From the heavens the stars, too, fought;
   from their courses they fought against Sisera.

21The Wadi Kishon swept them away;
   a wadi . . ., the Kishon.
22Then the hoofs of the horses pounded,
   with the dashing, dashing of his steeds.

23"Curse Meroz," says the LORD,
   "hurl a curse at its inhabitants!
For they came not to my help,
   as warriors to the help of the LORD."

Judges 5 is the song of Deborah, the retelling of the story in poetry. It is a rule of thumb that when a story appears twice—once in prose and once in poetry—the poetic version is older. The song of Deborah is thus the older version of the story, one of the oldest texts in the Bible itself.

In the song, Deborah is clearly presented as the leader. She is the one who rose up, "a mother in Israel," to deliver her people (5:7). Her heart went with the warriors; they were with her as well as was Barak (5:9, 15). The two of them take up their respective roles in the Holy War drama: Barak leads the battle, Deborah leads the victory song (5:12; cf. Exodus 15).

In the period of the judges (ca. 1250 B.C.E.) the Israelites had no central leader and no capital city. Their form of government can be compared to the government of the United States under the Articles of Confederation (1777–1788) when the rights of the states were primary. In Israel the rights of the tribes were primary. The twelve tribes were united by the covenant, symbolized by the ark of the covenant. There was no central sanctuary. The ark of the covenant moved from shrine to shrine. Wherever it was, there was Israel's official place of prayer and center of power.

The twelve judges are tribal leaders, not leaders of all Israel. A complaint continually made by them is that only a few neighboring tribes can be summoned to help in any crisis. The same complaint is registered in Deborah's song (5:14-18). Deborah, however, manages to muster six tribes—Ephraim, Benjamin, Manasseh, Zebulun, Issachar, and Naphtali—the largest number gathered by any of the twelve judges. It is a testimony to the power of her leadership. The combined forces win a great victory "and the land was at rest for forty years" (5:31).

THE ASSASSIN

Judges 4:17-24

[17]Sisera, in the meantime, had fled on foot to the tent of Jael, wife of the Kenite Heber, since Jabin, king of Hazor, and the family of the Kenite Heber were at peace with one another. [18]Jael went out to meet Sisera and said to him, "Come in, my lord, come in with me; do not be afraid." So he went into her tent, and she covered him with a rug. [19]He said to her, "Please give me a little water to drink. I am thirsty." But she opened a jug of milk for him to drink, and then covered him over. [20]"Stand at the entrance of the tent," he said to her. "If anyone comes and asks, 'Is there someone here?' say, 'No!'" [21]"Instead Jael, wife of Heber, got a tent peg and took a mallet in her hand. While Sisera was sound asleep, she stealthily approached him and drove the peg through his temple down into the ground, so that he perished in death. [22]Then when Barak came in pursuit of Sisera, Jael went out to meet him and said to him, "Come, I will show you the man you seek." So he went in with her, and there lay Sisera dead, with the tent peg through his temple.

[23]Thus on that day God humbled the Canaanite king, Jabin, before the Israelites; [24]their power weighed ever heavier upon him, till at length they destroyed the Canaanite king, Jabin.

Deborah predicted that God would give the glory of victory to a woman (4:9). The woman is not Deborah herself but Jael. Women rarely appear alone in the Bible. For good or for ill their stories are woven together. So, too, Deborah and Jael. The victory belongs to them both.

Jael, whose name means "mountain goat," is introduced as "the wife of the Kenite Heber." The Kenites were a group of metalworking nomads, identified as relatives of Moses (Judg 4:11; cf. Num 10:29). The family of Heber has made peace with the Canaanite king Jabin. Sisera, therefore, could expect to be protected in Heber's tent.

Jael takes the initiative in the encounter with Sisera. She goes out to meet him, invites him into the tent, and takes very good care of him! When he asks for water, she gives milk. She covers him twice (4:18, 19). Apparently her solicitude lulls Sisera into trusting her. He appoints her sentinel to guard the entrance of the tent while he sleeps. "Instead Jael, wife of Heber, got a tent peg" and killed Sisera. The murder is particularly gruesome. She kills him with the tent peg, driving it into his temple or possibly into his open mouth.

When Barak arrives, Jael greets him exactly as she greeted Sisera and brings him into her tent to see the results of her action. He is too late. She has done his work for him. She has destroyed the enemy of his people, a people not her own.

Judges 5:24-31

24Blessed among women be Jael,
  blessed among tent-dwelling women.
25He asked for water, she gave him milk;
  in a princely bowl she offered curds.
26With her left hand she reached for the peg,
  with her right, for the workman's mallet.

She hammered Sisera, crushed his head;
  she smashed, stove in his temple.
27At her feet he sank down, fell, lay still;
  down at her feet he sank and fell;
  where he sank down, there he fell, slain.

28From the window peered down and wailed
  the mother of Sisera, from the lattice:
"Why is his chariot so long in coming?

why are the hoofbeats of his chariots delayed?"
29The wisest of her princesses answers her,
 and she, too, keeps answering herself:
30"They must be dividing the spoil they took:
 there must be a damsel or two for each man,
Spoils of dyed cloth as Sisera's spoil,
 an ornate shawl or two for me in the spoil."
31May all your enemies perish thus, O LORD!
 but your friends be as the sun rising in its might!

The second half of Deborah's song is devoted to Jael's deed. She is introduced at the beginning of the song. "In the days of Shamgar, son of Anath, in the days of Jael, caravans ceased" (Judg 5:6).3 The stories of Shamgar (Judg 3:31) and Jael surround the story of Deborah.

The story of Jael's action begins with a beatitude: "Blessed among women be Jael" (5:24). Only two other biblical women are hailed as "blessed among women": Judith (Jdt 13:18) and Mary (Luke 1:42). All three are instrumental in the salvation of the people and in the destruction of the people's enemy. The following verses describe Sisera's death with grisly cheer. Jael "hammered," "crushed," "smashed," "stove in." Sisera "sank down, fell, lay still," "sank and fell," "sank down," "fell, slain." There is no doubt of Sisera's fate; there is no doubt of the poet's loyalty. Jael is a hero! The song of Deborah tells her story with obvious delight.

The vocabulary of verse 27 is suggestive of other realities surrounding war and the relationship between men and women. Rape is often a consequence of war for women. But Sisera does not enter Jael's tent to rape her; instead his fall between her legs is his undoing. Sisera "sinks down" (kneels/crouches), "falls," and "lies down between Jael's feet" (or between her legs). The Hebrew words, especially taken together, have a strong sexual connotation. The description is an allusion to rape; however, in this incident the man is the victim.

The vocabulary also suggests birth. In birth a woman crouches (cf. 1 Sam 4:19; Job 39:3); a child falls (cf. Isa 26:18)

3Sometimes *ya'el* (Jael) is emended to *'ol* (yoke), thus "slavery."

from between her legs. She gives the child milk; she covers it (cf. Judg 4:19; 5:25). Jael acts as a mother to Sisera, giving him milk and covering him for sleep. Unlike a child being born, however, Sisera is not entering life but leaving it.[4]

The violence of Jael's action offends us. It offends us doubly because the deed is done by a woman. What motivated this woman, a Kenite whose husband was allied with Jabin, to kill his army general? There may be two reasons. First, if Sisera is fleeing in defeat, the Israelite army cannot be far behind. A grisly fate awaits a woman who shelters an enemy general in her tent.[5] Second, from the standpoint of the Book of Judges, the heroes are those who deliver the people from the enemy— usually by military action, sometimes by assassination (cf. Ehud in Judg 2:12-30). Jael is praised as a hero by these standards.

JEPHTHAH'S DAUGHTER

Judges 11:29-40

[29]The spirit of the LORD came upon Jephthah. He passed through Gilead and Manasseh, and through Mizpah-Gilead as well, and from there he went on to the Ammonites. [30]Jephthah made a vow to the LORD. "If you deliver the Ammonites into my power," he said, [31]"whoever comes out of the doors of my house to meet me when I return in triumph from the Ammonites shall belong to the LORD. I shall offer him up as a holocaust."

[32]Jephthah then went on to the Ammonites to fight against them, and the LORD delivered them into his power, [33]so that he inflicted a severe defeat on them, from Aroer to the approach of Minnith (twenty cities in all) and as far as Abel-keramin. Thus were the Ammonites brought into subjection by the Israelites. [34]When Jephthah returned to his house in Mizpah, it was his daughter who came forth, playing the

[4]The interweaving of mother imagery is striking. Deborah is "a mother in Israel" (5:7). Jael "mothers" Sisera, while his own mother awaits his return (5:28).

[5]See the fate Sisera's princesses suggest for Israel's women: literally, "a womb or two for each man" (5:30).

tambourines and dancing. She was an only child: he had neither son nor daughter besides her. 35When he saw her, he rent his garments and said, "Alas, daughter, you have struck me down and brought calamity upon me. For I have made a vow to the LORD and I cannot retract." 36"Father," she replied, "you have made a vow to the LORD. Do with me as you have vowed, because the LORD has wrought vengeance for you on your enemies the Ammonites." 37Then she said to her father, "Let me have this favor. Spare me for two months, that I may go off down the mountains to mourn my virginity with my companions." 38"Go," he replied, and sent her away for two months. So she departed with her companions and mourned her virginity on the mountains. 39At the end of the two months she returned to her father, who did to her as he had vowed. She had not been intimate with man. It then became a custom in Israel 40for Israelite women to go yearly to mourn the daughter of Jephthah the Gileadite for four days of the year.

Jephthah is another judge-hero, called to deliver his people from a threatening enemy. Like most of the other judges, he performs this task through military victory. His story is remembered, however, not so much because of his own exploits, but because of his daughter.

Two things happen as Jephthah is going out to battle. First of all, the spirit of the Lord comes upon him. This is a common phrase in the Book of Judges (3:10; 11:29; 14:6, 19; 15:14; cf. 6:34; 13:25). It signifies God's power on the chosen hero; his victory will be God's. But apparently this is not enough for Jephthah. Secondly, he makes a vow, promising God a sacrifice if God will give him the victory. The victim of the sacrifice will be the first living thing—human or animal—who meets him after the victory.

Jephthah's vow presents several problems. It seems he does not trust God and finds it necessary to bargain or bribe. Is he insecure because of his tenuous position in the family? It also appears that he is willing to make a human sacrifice. Human sacrifice is nowhere approved in the Bible. Abraham is stopped from sacrificing his son (Gen 22:12-13). Various kings are severely criticized for sacrificing children (2 Kings 16:3; 21:6; 2 Chr 28:3; 33:6). The law forbids human sacrifice

(Lev 18:21; 20:2-5; Deut 12:31). The other nations are scorned because they practice it (2 Kings 17:31; Ps 106:34-38). The prophets rail against it (Jer 7:31; 19:5; Ezek 16:20-21; 20:31). But Jephthah's vow allows for, even suggests, a human sacrifice.

A third dilemma is presented by the vow. Ancient peoples, including Israel, had a great respect for the power of the spoken word. A word once spoken took on its own power. Isaac's blessing of Jacob, once spoken, cannot be taken back (Gen 27:37). The content of curses was often disguised, for fear their spoken words might rebound on the speaker (e.g., Ruth 1:17; 1 Sam 3:17; 14:44). Jephthah has spoken his vow; it cannot be taken back.

The designated victim of the sacrifice is his daughter, his only child. She emerges from the house first, carrying out the woman's role in victory. Like Miriam she leads the celebration, playing the tambourines and dancing (Exod 15:20; cf. 1 Sam 18:6; Jdt 15:12–16:1). But her celebration is her death sentence. Jephthah's exclamation upon seeing her is ironic: "Alas, daughter, *you* have struck me down and brought calamity upon me" (11:35, emphasis mine). The disaster is her own fault; the blame for her death is laid upon her. Her father— bound by his vow—uses it to claim innocence.

The daughter surrenders to her father's vow. She asks only one favor, to go off with her companions to mourn her virginity. In a society where there is no belief in true life after death,[6] children are the one hope to live on and to be remembered. Virginity in such a situation is a curse. There will be no children. Her memory will be snuffed out with her life. She has not reckoned, however, on the interweaving of women's lives. Her death becomes the occasion for Israelite women to mourn her four days every year. She lives in their memory.

Jephthah's daughter is remembered by the women but forgotten in the rest of the biblical story. Her father Jephthah is held up by Samuel as an example of those God sent to deliver

[6]The common belief in ancient Israel was that all the dead went to a place called Sheol. Existence in Sheol was at best shadowy: no joy nor sorrow; no pleasure nor pain; no memory nor communication; no sensory experience (cf. Job 3:13-19). There was some suggestion that God might be present in Sheol, but most did not believe it (cf. Ps 88:11-13).

Israel (1 Sam 12:11). He is held up by the author of the Letter to the Hebrews as an example of faith and righteousness (Heb 11:32-33). His daughter is not mentioned again. But is Jephthah really a hero? Can we bear to consider him as such?

Should Jephthah's daughter have surrendered to her horrible death? That question has exercised commentators, especially in this century. Some see her as a model of obedience; many assume that she had no choice. She has been criticized for not defying such a stupid vow. Recently it has also been suggested that the point of her story is the women's yearly celebration mentioned in verse 40. Her story belongs to a (hypothetical) rite of passage, a story of death to childhood at the beginning of puberty.

Jephthah's daughter remains a tragic figure in biblical literature. She is sacrificed for her father's victory, her father's glory, her father's religion. Her father will not back down on his vow. Neither, it seems, will God. This time there is no ram in the thicket, no change of plan (cf. Gen 22:13; 1 Sam 14:24-26, 43-45). Jephthah's daughter dies as a burnt offering, the victim of a vow. Israel's deliverance is bought at the price of her life.

THE WOMEN AROUND SAMSON

SAMSON'S MOTHER

Judges 13:1-25

1The Israelites again offended the LORD, who therefore delivered them into the power of the Philistines for forty years.

2There was a certain man from Zorah, of the clan of the Danites, whose name was Manoah. His wife was barren and had borne no children. 3An angel of the LORD appeared to the woman and said to her, "Though you are barren and have had no children, yet you will conceive and bear a son. 4Now, then, be careful to take no wine or strong drink and to eat nothing unclean. 5As for the son you will conceive and bear, no razor shall touch his head, for this boy is to be consecrated to God from the womb. It is he who will begin the deliverance of Israel from the power of the Philistines."

6The woman went and told her husband, "A man of God came to me; he had the appearance of an angel of God, terrible indeed. I did not ask him where he came from, nor did he tell me his name. 7But he said to me, 'You will be with child and will bear a son. So take neither wine nor strong drink, and eat nothing unclean. For the boy shall be consecrated to God from the womb, until the day of his death.'" 8Manoah then prayed to the LORD. "O LORD, I beseech you," he said, "may the man of God whom you sent, return to us to teach us what to do for the boy who will be born."

9God heard the prayer of Manoah, and the angel of God came again to the woman as she was sitting in the field. Since her husband Manoah was not with her, 10the woman ran in haste and told her husband. "The man who came to me the other day has appeared to me," she said to him; 11so Manoah got up and followed his wife. When he reached the man, he said to him, "Are you the one who spoke to my wife?" "Yes," he answered. 12Then Manoah asked, "Now, when that which you say comes true, what are we expected to do for the boy?" 13The angel of the LORD answered Manoah, "Your wife is to abstain from all the things of which I spoke to her. 14She must not eat anything that comes from the vine, nor take wine or strong drink, nor eat anything unclean. Let her observe all that I have commanded her." 15Then Manoah said to the angel of the LORD, "Can we persuade you to stay, while we prepare a kid for you?" 16But the angel of the LORD answered Manoah, "Although you press me, I will not partake of your food. But if you will, you may offer a holocaust to the LORD." Not knowing that it was the angel of the LORD, 17Manoah said to him, "What is your name, that we may honor you when your words come true?" 18The angel of the LORD answered him, "Why do you ask my name, which is mysterious?" 19Then Manoah took the kid with a cereal offering and offered it on the rock to the LORD, whose works are mysteries. While Manoah and his wife were looking on, 20as the flame rose to the sky from the altar, the angel of the LORD ascended in the flame of the altar. When Manoah and his wife saw this, they fell prostrate to the ground; 21but the angel of the LORD was seen no more by Manoah and his wife. Then Manoah, realizing that it was the angel of the LORD, 22said to his wife, "We will certainly die, for we have seen God." 23But his wife pointed out to him, "If the LORD had meant to kill us, he would not have accepted a holocaust and cereal offering from our hands! Nor would he have let us see all this just now, or hear what we have heard."

24The woman bore a son and named him Samson. The boy grew up and the LORD blessed him; 25the spirit of the LORD first stirred him in Mahaneh-dan, which is between Zorah and Eshtaol.

The Book of Judges borrows many patterns and themes from earlier narratives. Within the story of Samson, which is based on the common pattern of judge stories,7 there are other smaller forms. The way the forms are used reveals the meaning in the story. One such form is found in Judges 13, which is an extended announcement of birth form.8 Within this chapter we also find the barren wife theme, a description of the nazirite vow, and the encounter between human beings and the angel of the Lord. Throughout the chapter, the wife of Manoah is a central figure.

The use of the announcement of birth form signals the importance of this child. God will bless the Israelites through him and deliver them from their enemies. The announcement of birth begins with the appearance of the angel of the Lord to the wife of Manoah. The second element of the form, however, is missing: she expresses no fear. In fact, the only expression of fear in the whole chapter comes from her husband when he finally realizes that this is indeed an angel of the Lord (13:21-22). The form continues with the third element, the message. The angel tells Manoah's wife that she will bear a son and reveals to her the son's future mission. There is no mention of the son's name.

At this point the form is stretched. The conversation between the angel and the woman ends and she goes to report the event to Manoah. He asks for a second appearance which God grants. The message is repeated and Manoah suggests a sacrifice. The only hint of an objection (the fourth element of the form) is Manoah's constant questioning that ends with a request for the angel's name. The request is refused but the sacrifice is accepted. The angel ascends within the sacrificial flame (a sign? the sixth element) and Manoah is sure they will die. The reassurance (fifth element) comes, not from the angel,

---

7See the description of the pattern in the commentary on Deborah.
8See the description of this form in the commentary on Sarah.

but from the woman: If the Lord were going to kill us, our sacrifice would not have been accepted and we would not have been given this message. The announcement of birth is fulfilled: The woman bears a son and names him Samson. The spirit of the Lord comes upon him (13:25; cf. 14:6, 19; 15:14).

The variation in the form alerts us to the presence of a deeper message. The effect of the subtle changes is to emphasize the importance of the woman. We expect someone to object to the impending birth, but this woman does not object. The second appearance of the angel, this time to the woman with her husband, provides the opportunity for an objection from her husband. We also expect a reassurance. Ordinarily it would come from the angel, but in this story it comes from the woman. These variations make clear the faith of this extraordinary woman and her willingness to be a channel of God's care for the people. In the story of Samson no other character shows such faith and obedience to God.

Appearances of angels often strike terror in human beings. There is a tradition that no human being can see the face of God (even reflected on the face of an angel) and live. Because of this tradition, Manoah thinks they will die. However, there are no stories of anyone dying from such a vision, but many stories of amazement that life continues: Hagar (Gen 16:13); Jacob (Gen 32:31); the Sinai community (Exod 20:19; cf. Deut 4:33). Manoah does not understand the messenger of God, but his wife does.

It is the woman who is entrusted with the child's nazirite vow (13:4-5, 7, 13-14). A nazirite vow is a special consecration to God. The signs of this consecration are: abstaining from strong drink, avoiding all contact with dead bodies, and not cutting the hair (cf. Num 6:2-8).[9] This vow will be very important in the life of Samson (cf. Judg 16). Because it is a consecration from the womb, Samson's mother keeps the vow for him as long as she carries him. She is more faithful to it than Samson will be. She is the one to whom the instructions for the vow are given. She repeats them to her husband as the angel will later do. She is responsible for the vow.

[9]Samuel (1 Sam 1:11, 22-28) and John the Baptist (Luke 1:13-15) were also nazirites for life. Paul made a temporary nazirite vow (Acts 18:18).

Manoah's wife is the primary recipient of the announcement of birth, just as Hagar was (Gen 16:7-16). Even in the second appearance, the angel appears to her first. She is an example of faith: she listens to the word of God mediated through the angel; she builds her life around that word. She is another barren wife, in the tradition of Sarah, Rebekah, and Rachel. It is she who recognizes the angel (13:6) and she who understands the significance of the message. They will not die, but live to carry out God's plan. It is through this nameless woman that God chooses to work. It is only at the end of his life that her son, Samson, will finally live up to her example.

SAMSON'S WIFE

Judges 14:1-4

> [1]Samson went down to Timnah and saw there one of the Philistine women. [2]On his return he told his father and mother, "There is a Philistine woman I saw in Timnah whom I wish you to get as a wife for me." [3]His father and mother said to him, "Can you find no wife among your kinsfolk or among all our people, that you must go and take a wife from the uncircumcised Philistines?" But Samson answered his father, "Get her for me, for she pleases me." [4]Now his father and mother did not know that this had been brought about by the LORD, who was providing an opportunity against the Philistines; for at that time they had dominion over Israel.

The introduction to the story of Samson's marriage reveals two of his character flaws: he is demanding and there is no discipline in his desire for a woman. Samson sees a Philistine woman and wants her. In this period (1250 B.C.E.–1000 B.C.E.) the Philistines were Israel's greatest enemy. The two peoples were locked in a mortal struggle for possession of the land. The Philistines had the technological advantage; they knew how to smelt iron. But Samson wants this woman and nothing will stand in his way. His parents try to persuade him to find "a nice girl in the neighborhood." But he says to his father, "Get her for me." His attitude warns that this marriage will be difficult.

Judges 14:5-20

⁵So Samson went down to Timnah with his father and mother. When they had come to the vineyards of Timnah, a young lion came roaring to meet him. ⁶But the spirit of the LORD came upon Samson, and although he had no weapons, he tore the lion in pieces as one tears a kid. ⁷However, on the journey to speak for the woman, he did not mention to his father or mother what he had done. ⁸Later, when he returned to marry the woman who pleased him, he stepped aside to look at the remains of the lion and found a swarm of bees and honey in the lion's carcass. ⁹So he scooped the honey out into his palms and ate it as he went along. When he came to his father and mother, he gave them some to eat, without telling them that he had scooped the honey from the lion's carcass.

¹⁰His father also went down to the woman, and Samson gave a banquet there, since it was customary for the young men to do this. ¹¹When they met him, they brought thirty men to be his companions. ¹²Samson said to them, "Let me propose a riddle to you. If within the seven days of the feast you solve it for me successfully, I will give you thirty linen tunics and thirty sets of garments. ¹³But if you cannot answer it for me, you must give me thirty tunics and thirty sets of garments." "Propose your riddle," they responded; "we will listen to it." ¹⁴So he said to them,

"Out of the eater came forth food,
    and out of the strong came forth sweetness."

After three days' failure to answer the riddle, ¹⁵they said on the fourth day to Samson's wife, "Coax your husband to answer the riddle for us, or we will burn you and your family. Did you invite us here to reduce us to poverty?" ¹⁶At Samson's side, his wife wept and said, "You must hate me; you do not love me, for you have proposed a riddle to my countrymen, but have not told me the answer." He said to her, "If I have not told it even to my father or my mother, must I tell it to you?" ¹⁷But she wept beside him during the seven days the feast lasted. On the seventh day, since she importuned him, he told her the answer, and she explained the riddle to her countrymen.

¹⁸On the seventh day, before the sun set, the men of the city said to him,

"What is sweeter than honey,
   and what is stronger than a lion?"

He replied to them,

"If you had not plowed with my heifer,
   you would not have solved my riddle."

[19]The spirit of the LORD came upon him, and he went down
to Ashkelon, where he killed thirty of their men and de-
spoiled them; he gave their garments to those who had answered the riddle. Then he went off to his own family in
anger, [20]and Samson's wife was married to the one who had
been best man at his wedding.

Samson has his way and the wedding takes place. During
the celebration he makes a wager. He thinks he cannot lose.
The riddle he proposes is based, not on common human experience, but on his own particular experience. No one could
know the answer. In this sense the wager is unfair. The young
Philistine men find that indeed they cannot solve the riddle by
wit, so they turn to another method, pressuring the bride.
They threaten her life and the lives of her family. The woman
is put in an impossible situation. She has to choose between
the demands of her own people and loyalty to her new husband. She has to consider whether she and her family will be
protected by Samson or by the Philistines. Where should her
loyalty be? Where is safety for her?
   Whether out of fear or loyalty, she chooses to trust her own
people, the Philistines. She coaxes the solution from Samson
and reveals the secret to her countrymen. They answer Samson
riddle for riddle. Their riddle demonstrates knowledge of his
experience with the honeycomb in the carcass of the lion.
(Note that in touching the lion's carcass Samson has already
broken his nazirite vow.) Samson knows that his bride has to
be the source of the information. His response again reveals
his character. He kills thirty men and pays off his wager with
their clothes. Then he returns home in anger.
   What of the bride? Her wedding has turned to disaster. She
was promised in marriage to a violent, demanding man from
an enemy people. He used the wedding celebration to insti-
gate a fight between his people and hers. She is forced to

choose sides. Her choice wins the wager for some of her countrymen, but causes the death of others. With the angry departure of her bridegroom, she is given in marriage to another man, probably still without consideration for her feelings. She is a tragic figure, the victim of a ruthless culture.

Judges 15:1-8

¹After some time, in the season of the wheat harvest, Samson visited his wife, bringing a kid. But when he said, "Let me be with my wife in private," her father would not let him enter, ²saying, "I thought it certain you wished to repudiate her; so I gave her to your best man. Her younger sister is more beautiful than she; you may have her instead." ³Samson said to them, "This time the Philistines cannot blame me if I harm them." ⁴So Samson left and caught three hundred foxes. Turning them tail to tail, he tied between each pair of tails one of the torches he had at hand. ⁵He then kindled the torches and set the foxes loose in the standing grain of the Philistines, thus burning both the shocks and the standing grain, and the vineyards and olive orchards as well.

⁶When the Philistines asked who had done this, they were told, "Samson, the son-in-law of the Timnite, because his wife was taken and given to his best man." So the Philistines went up and destroyed her and her family by fire. ⁷Samson said to them, "If this is how you act, I will not stop until I have taken revenge on you." ⁸And with repeated blows, he inflicted a great slaughter on them. Then he went down and remained in a cavern of the cliff of Etam.

Samson has not forgotten his bride. After some time he returns to Timnah to consummate his marriage. The woman's father informs him that it is too late; she is married to another man. Instead, he offers Samson another woman, his younger daughter. Samson again becomes enraged. He burns the whole wheat harvest along with the vineyards and olive orchards. In retaliation the Philistines carry out the threat made earlier (Judg 14:15). They burn his would-be bride along with her whole family. Samson's response is to slaughter yet more Philistines.

Thus this woman and her family suffer a horrible death. Her only active part in the tragedy was to make a choice for the Philistines, her own people, and against Samson, her husband. The choice was made under compulsion; either choice would have destroyed her. She is destroyed in the enmity between two peoples. Her death symbolizes the subjugation of the Philistines by the Israelites.

DELILAH

Judges 16:1-22

1Once Samson went to Gaza, where he saw a harlot and visited her. 2Informed that Samson had come there, the men of Gaza surrounded him with an ambush at the city gate all night long. And all the night they waited, saying, "Tomorrow morning we will kill him." 3Samson rested there until midnight. Then he rose, seized the doors of the city gate and the two gateposts, and tore them loose, bar and all. He hoisted them on his shoulders and carried them to the top of the ridge opposite Hebron.

4After that he fell in love with a woman in the Wadi Sorek whose name was Delilah. 5The lords of the Philistines came to her and said, "Beguile him and find out the secret of his great strength, and how we may overcome and bind him so as to keep him helpless. We will each give you eleven hundred shekels of silver."

6So Delilah said to Samson, "Tell me the secret of your great strength and how you may be bound so as to be kept helpless." 7"If they bind me with seven fresh bowstrings which have not dried," Samson answered her, "I shall be as weak as any other man." 8So the lords of the Philistines brought her seven fresh bowstrings which had not dried, and she bound him with them. 9She had men lying in wait in the chamber and so she said to him, "The Philistines are upon you, Samson!" But he snapped the strings as a thread of tow is severed by a whiff of flame; and the secret of his strength remained unknown.

10Delilah said to Samson, "You have mocked me and told me lies. Now tell me how you may be bound." 11"If they bind me tight with new ropes, with which no work has been done," he answered her, "I shall be as weak as any other man." ¹²So Delilah took new ropes and bound him with them. Then she said to him, "The Philistines are upon you, Samson!" For there were men lying in wait in the chamber. But he snapped them off his arms like thread.

¹³Delilah said to Samson again, "Up to now you have mocked me and told me lies. Tell me how you may be bound." He said to her, "If you weave my seven locks of hair into the web and fasten them with the pin, I shall be as weak as any other man." ¹⁴So while he slept, Delilah wove his seven locks of hair into the web, and fastened them in with the pin. Then she said, "The Philistines are upon you, Samson!" Awakening from his sleep, he pulled out both the weaver's pin and the web.

¹⁵Then she said to him, "How can you say that you love me when you do not confide in me? Three times already you have mocked me, and not told me the secret of your great strength!" ¹⁶She importuned him continually and vexed him with her complaints till he was deathly weary of them. ¹⁷So he took her completely into his confidence and told her, "No razor has touched my head, for I have been consecrated to God from my mother's womb. If I am shaved, my strength will leave me, and I shall be as weak as any other man." ¹⁸When Delilah saw that he had taken her completely into his confidence, she summoned the lords of the Philistines, saying, "Come up this time, for he has opened his heart to me." So the lords of the Philistines came and brought up the money with them. ¹⁹She had him sleep on her lap, and called for a man who shaved off his seven locks of hair. Then she began to mistreat him, for his strength had left him. ²⁰When she said, "The Philistines are upon you, Samson!", and he woke from his sleep, he thought he could make good his escape as he had done time and again, for he did not realize that the LORD had left him. ²¹But the Philistines seized him and gouged out his eyes. Then they brought him down to Gaza and bound him with bronze fetters, and he was put to grinding in the prison. ²²But the hair of his head began to grow as soon as it was shaved off.

Chapter sixteen begins with a story of Samson and a harlot. The narrative continues to remind us of Samson's weakness for women. The brief story of the harlot introduces the story of Delilah, a woman who proves to be stronger than Samson.

Delilah is also a Philistine woman. In this story of many women, she is the only one whom Samson is said to love. She is placed in a situation similar to that of Samson's bride. The Philistines want to use her to gain the secret of Samson's strength. They do not threaten her as they did the bride, however. Instead, they promise her a great deal of money.

Three times Delilah attempts to learn Samson's secret. Each time the Philistines act on the information she gives them. Each time Samson has deceived her. Thus when she begs him the fourth time to reveal the secret to her, he must know that she will again betray him to the Philistines. But Samson cannot resist her pleading, just as he could not resist the pleading of his bride. Both women pose the question as a test of love: "How can you say that you love me when you do not confide in me?" (16:15; cf. 14:16). Finally Samson "opens his heart" to Delilah. His strength comes from his consecration to God; his long hair is the sign of that consecration. A fourth time Delilah summons the Philistines who cut his hair, blind him, and imprison him. It seems the end of Samson's strength. But his hair grows back; his strength returns. One day when the Philistines are celebrating in the temple of their god Dagon, they chain Samson between two of the supporting columns. After a prayer to God for strength, he pulls down the columns and with them the temple. He destroys more Philistines with his death than in his lifetime (Judg 16:23-30).

Delilah is often seen as a heartless woman who uses the power of love and sexuality to destroy a man, a woman to whom money is worth more than love. It is possible, however, that she, a Philistine woman, knows the fate of the other Philistine woman who loved Samson. Perhaps she betrays Samson in order to save her own life. Perhaps her motive is loyalty to her own people. If this story were told by the Philistines, she would be seen as a hero. She betrays Samson to save her people just as Judith killed Holofernes to save hers. The story does not report her reasons. She is, however, the most complex and developed female character in the story of Samson.

5. More Women of Israel's Early Tribes

Suggested readings: Book of Ruth; 1 Samuel 1–2

THREE WIDOWS: ORPAH, NAOMI, AND RUTH

Three women are introduced in the first chapter of the Book of Ruth: Naomi, Ruth, and Orpah. They are the survivors of the family of Elimilech. All the men have died. The three women face the same problem. Left with neither husband nor sons, each woman is doomed to poverty and possible starvation. Her options are re-marriage, begging, or prostitution. Israelite society expected a widow to marry within the family of her dead husband[1] or to return to her father's house. The law commanded faithful Israelites to be charitable to widows, along with strangers and orphans (cf. Deut 14:28-29; 24:17-21), but there were no honorable ways for a woman alone to earn her own living.

ORPAH: THE DAUGHTER-IN-LAW

Ruth 1:1-22

[1]Once in the time of the judges there was a famine in the land; so a man from Bethlehem of Judah departed with his wife and two sons to reside on the plateau of Moab. [2]The man was named Elimelech, his wife Naomi, and his sons Mahlon and Chilion; they were Ephrathites from Bethlehem of Judah. Some time after their arrival on the Moabite plateau, [3]Elimelech, the husband of Naomi, died, and she

---

[1]See the discussion of levirate marriage in the commentary on Tamar (Genesis 38).

was left with her two sons, 4who married Moabite women, one named Orpah, the other Ruth. When they had lived there about ten years, 5both Mahlon and Chilion died also, and the woman was left with neither her two sons nor her husband. 6She then made ready to go back from the plateau of Moab because word reached her there that the LORD had visited his people and given them food.

7She and her two daughters-in-law left the place where they had been living. Then as they were on the road back to the land of Judah, 8Naomi said to her two daughters-in-law, "Go back, each of you, to your mother's house! May the LORD be kind to you as you were to the departed and to me! 9May the LORD grant each of you a husband and a home in which you will find rest." She kissed them good-by, but they wept with loud sobs, 10and told her they would return with her to her people. 11"Go back, my daughters!" said Naomi. "Why should you come with me? Have I other sons in my womb who may become your husbands? 12Go back, my daughters! Go, for I am too old to marry again. And even if I could offer any hopes, or if tonight I had a husband or had borne sons, 13would you then wait and deprive yourselves of husbands until those sons grew up? No, my daughters! my lot is too bitter for you, because the LORD has extended his hand against me." 14Again they sobbed aloud and wept; and Orpah kissed her mother-in-law good-by, but Ruth stayed with her.

15"See now!" she said, "your sister-in-law has gone back to her people and her god. Go back after your sister-in-law!" 16But Ruth said, "Do not ask me to abandon or forsake you! for wherever you go I will go, wherever you lodge I will lodge, your people shall be my people, and your God my God. 17Wherever you die I will die, and there be buried. May the LORD do so and so to me, and more besides, if aught but death separates me from you!" 18Naomi then ceased to urge her, for she saw she was determined to go with her.

19So they went on together till they reached Bethlehem. On their arrival there, the whole city was astir over them, and the women asked, "Can this be Naomi?" 20But she said to them, "Do not call me Naomi. Call me Mara, for the Almighty has made it very bitter for me. 21I went away with an abundance, but the LORD has brought me back destitute. Why should you call me Naomi, since the LORD has pronounced against me and the Almighty has brought evil upon me?" 22Thus it was that Naomi returned with the Moabite daughter-in-law, Ruth, who accompanied her back from the plateau of Moab. They arrived in Bethlehem at the beginning of the barley harvest.

Orpah is a Moabite woman, Chilion's widow, the daughter-in-law of Elimilech and Naomi. She has risked marriage with a foreigner. Along with the misery of her own childlessness, she has suffered the death of her husband, her father-in-law, and her brother-in-law. As the story opens, she is beginning a journey with her mother-in-law to a strange place where her people are not welcome (cf. Deut 23:4-7).

The mother-in-law, Naomi, insists that the two daughters-in-law should return home. She cannot support them; she has no other sons who can marry them. She can promise them nothing in her own land. She sends them back to their *mother's* house (1:8), an unusual designation in a society where a house normally belonged to the father. Orpah heeds her mother-in-law's words and in sorrow kisses her goodbye. She returns to the land of Moab.

Because the story follows the life of Ruth, Orpah has often been neglected or even scorned by commentators. Her own virtues, however, deserve to be considered. She acts out of genuine love for her mother-in-law. She remains with Naomi after her husband's death; she begins the journey back to her husband's native land. There is no future for her in either of these actions. What motive can there be except love for the family into which she has married?

She heeds the wisdom of her mother-in-law and obeys her. She will not be a burden to Naomi. She returns to her mother's house. The departure with tears and kisses certainly demonstrates the love between Orpah and Naomi.

Orpah is a good daughter-in-law—loving, caring, and obedient toward her mother-in-law Naomi.

NAOMI: THE MOTHER-IN-LAW

Ruth 2:1-23

1Naomi had a prominent kinsman named Boaz, of the clan of her husband Elimelech. 2Ruth the Moabite said to Naomi,

"Let me go and glean ears of grain in the field of anyone who will allow me that favor." Naomi said to her, "Go, my daughter," ³and she went. The field she entered to glean after the harvesters happened to be the section belonging to Boaz of the clan of Elimelech. ⁴Boaz himself came from Bethlehem and said to the harvesters, "The LORD be with you!" and they replied, "The LORD bless you!" ⁵Boaz asked the overseer of his harvesters, "Whose girl is this?" ⁶The overseer of the harvesters answered, "She is the Moabite girl who returned from the plateau of Moab with Naomi. ⁷She asked leave to gather the gleanings into sheaves after the harvesters; and ever since she came this morning she has remained here until now, with scarcely a moment's rest."

⁸Boaz said to Ruth, "Listen, my daughter! Do not go to glean in anyone else's field; you are not to leave here. Stay here with my women servants. ⁹Watch to see which field is to be harvested, and follow them; I have commanded the young men to do you no harm. When you are thirsty, you may go and drink from the vessels the young men have filled." ¹⁰Casting herself prostrate upon the ground, she said to him, "Why should I, a foreigner, be favored with your notice?" ¹¹Boaz answered her: "I have had a complete account of what you have done for your mother-in-law after your husband's death; you have left your father and your mother and the land of your birth, and have come to a people whom you did not know previously. ¹²May the LORD reward what you have done! May you receive a full reward from the LORD, the God of Israel, under whose wings you have come for refuge." ¹³She said, "May I prove worthy of your kindness, my lord: you have comforted me, your servant, with your consoling words; would indeed that I were a servant of yours!" ¹⁴At mealtime Boaz said to her, "Come here and have some food; dip your bread in the sauce." Then as she sat near the reapers, he handed her some roasted grain and she ate her fill and had some left over. ¹⁵She rose to glean, and Boaz instructed his servants to let her glean among the sheaves themselves without scolding her, ¹⁶and even to let drop some handfuls and leave them for her to glean without being rebuked.

¹⁷She gleaned in the field until evening, and when she beat out what she had gleaned it came to about an ephah of barley, ¹⁸which she took into the city and showed to her

mother-in-law. Next she brought out and gave her what she had left over from lunch. [19]So her mother-in-law said to her, "Where did you glean today? Where did you go to work? May he who took notice of you be blessed!" Then she told her mother-in-law with whom she had worked. "The man at whose place I worked today is named Boaz," she said. [20]"May he be blessed by the LORD, who is ever merciful to the living and to the dead," Naomi exclaimed to her daughter-in-law; and she continued, "He is a relative of ours, one of our next of kin." [21]"He even told me," added Ruth the Moabite, "that I should stay with his servants until they complete his entire harvest." [22]"You would do well, my dear," Naomi rejoined, "to go out with his servants; for in someone else's field you might be insulted." [23]So she stayed gleaning with the servants of Boaz until the end of the barley and wheat harvests.

Naomi is the primary actor in the story of Ruth. When she is introduced she seems to be a powerless person, a widow who has lost not only her husband but both her sons (Ruth 1:1-6). In addition, she is a sojourner in a strange land. All she has is the love and faithfulness of two daughters-in-law to whom she can offer nothing. Yet she is a competent, inventive woman who makes the best of whatever life offers her.

She returns to her home town of Bethlehem, accompanied by one daughter-in-law. The bitterness of her experience is revealed in her comment to the women of Bethlehem: "Do not call me Naomi [which means "pleasant"]. Call me Mara [which means "bitter"], for the Almighty has made it very bitter for me" (1:20). She lays the responsibility for her distress squarely at the feet of God. "The Almighty has brought evil upon me" (1:21).

Naomi's tragic situation does not cause her to give up, however. Throughout the story she is definitely the one in charge. Ruth asks her permission to glean and Naomi expects a full report when she returns. She immediately sees the opportunity with Boaz and plans the event at the threshing floor (3:1-6). Again, Ruth does just as her mother-in-law instructs and returns to report the results (3:16-17).

Naomi knows how to wait. After Ruth returns from the threshing floor, Naomi instructs, "Wait here, my daughter, until you learn what happens, for the man will not rest, but will settle the matter today" (3:18). At the end of the story, it is Naomi who is the beneficiary. The neighbor women say to Naomi, "Blessed is the LORD who has not failed to provide you today with an heir!" (4:14). She claims the child, placing him on her lap and becoming his nurse. The neighbor women name him Obed when they hear a grandson is born to Naomi (4:17).

Naomi weaves together the lives of all the characters in the story. She is wife, mother, mother-in-law. She is friend, so loved that one daughter-in-law refuses to leave her and the other sobs as she departs. She is relative to Boaz and knows his character. She is neighbor to the women of Bethlehem and they continue to be interested in her affairs. She is grand-mother to baby Obed and great-great-grandmother of King David. The story happens all around her and she is influential in shaping all its events. She is a woman of competence and wit.

RUTH

Ruth 3:1-18

¹When she was back with her mother-in-law, Naomi said to her, "My daughter, I must seek a home for you that will please you. ²Now is not Boaz, with whose servants you were, a relative of ours? This evening he will be winnowing barley at the threshing floor. ³So bathe and anoint yourself; then put on your best attire and go down to the threshing floor. Do not make yourself known to the man before he has finished eating and drinking. ⁴But when he lies down, take note of the place where he does so. Then go, uncover a place at his feet, and lie down. He will tell you what to do." ⁵"I will do whatever you advise," Ruth replied. ⁶So she went down to the threshing floor and did just as her mother-in-law had instructed her.

⁷Boaz ate and drank to his heart's content. Then when he went and lay down at the edge of the sheaves, she stole up, uncovered a place at his feet, and lay down. ⁸In the middle of the night, however, the man gave a start and turned around to find a woman lying at his feet. ⁹He asked, "Who are you?" And she replied, "I am your servant Ruth. Spread the corner of your cloak over me, for you are my next of

kin." 10He said, "May the LORD bless you, my daughter! You have been even more loyal now than before in not going after the young men, whether poor or rich. 11So be assured, daughter, I will do for you whatever you say; all my towns-people know you for a worthy woman. 12Now, though indeed I am closely related to you, you have another relative still closer. 13Stay as you are for tonight, and tomorrow, if he wishes to claim you, good! let him do so. But if he does not wish to claim you, as the LORD lives, I will claim you myself. Lie there until morning." 14So she lay at his feet until morning, but rose before men could recognize one another. Boaz said, "Let it not be known that this woman came to the threshing floor." 15Then he said to her, "Take off your cloak and hold it out." When she did so, he poured out six measures of barley, helped her lift the bundle, and left for the city.

16Ruth went home to her mother-in-law, who asked, "How have you fared, my daughter?" So she told her all the man had done for her, 17and concluded, "He gave me these six measures of barley because he did not wish me to come back to my mother-in-law empty-handed!" 18Naomi then said, "Wait here, my daughter, until you learn what happens, for the man will not rest, but will settle the matter today."

Ruth is the widowed daughter-in-law of a widowed mother-in-law, a woman surrounded by death. She is a foreigner in Israel. Worse, she is a Moabite. Deuteronomy prescribes, "No Ammonite or Moabite may ever be admitted into the community of the LORD, nor any descendants of theirs even to the tenth generation, because they would not succor you with food and water on your journey after you left Egypt, and because Moab hired Balaam, son of Beor, from Pethor in Aram Naharaim, to curse you; though the LORD, your God, would not listen to Balaam and turned his curse into a blessing for you, because he loves you. Never promote their peace and prosperity as long as you live" (Deut 23:4-7; cf. Neh 13:1-3, 23-25). There seems to be little Ruth can hope for.

She is undaunted by this situation, however. She faithfully follows her beloved mother-in-law. She speaks the words that have become a well-known testimony to undying love: "Wherever you go I will go, wherever you lodge I will lodge, your people shall be my people, and your God my God.

Wherever you die I will die, and there be buried. May the LORD do so and so to me, and more besides, if aught but death separates me from you" (Ruth 1:16-17). She goes to work to support herself and Naomi (2:2). She is diligent, working "with scarcely a moment's rest" (2:7). She is humble. When Boaz, the owner of the field, speaks kindly to her, she replies: "Why should I, a foreigner, be favored with your notice?" (2:10). She is generous. She brings her mother-in-law not only what she has gleaned, but even what she had saved from lunch (2:17-18). She is a gentle, kind, unassuming woman.

Ruth is also brave and daring. When Naomi conceives the plan to remind Boaz that he could fulfill the levirate obligation by marrying Ruth, she obeys without question. She does exactly what her mother-in-law suggests. She bathes and anoints herself, puts on her best clothes, and goes to the threshing floor at night. There she uncovers the sleeping Boaz and lies down at his feet. Her actions are hardly expected of a respectable woman! She also puts herself at considerable risk. How safe is a woman, a foreigner besides, alone at night at a threshing floor where the men have been drinking?

Boaz, however, has become her protector (cf. 2:8-9, 15). When she informs him that he is her next of kin, he blesses her. He credits her with *hesed,* the covenant virtue of loyal love, for heeding her mother-in-law rather than "going after the young men." He adds that the townspeople know that she is "a worthy woman." Even though she is a Moabite, daughter of a hated enemy, he finds that she observes the covenant and is worthy of being his wife.

Boaz needs to settle a prior claim; there is a still closer relative than he. So he sends Ruth away from the threshing floor before anyone can recognize her and spread gossip. But he does not send her home empty-handed. She returns to Naomi not only with the news, but with a cloak full of barley. Then with Naomi she waits while the men settle the legal matters.

HAPPY ENDING

Ruth 4:1-22

[1]Boaz went and took a seat at the gate; and when he saw the closer relative of whom he had spoken come along, he called

to him by name, "Come and sit beside me!" And he did so.
²Then Boaz picked out ten of the elders of the city and asked
them to sit nearby. When they had done this, ³he said to the
near relative: "Naomi, who has come back from the Moabite
plateau, is putting up for sale the piece of land that belonged
to our kinsman Elimelech. ⁴So I thought I would inform you,
bidding you before those here present, including the elders
of my people, to put in your claim for it if you wish to acquire it as next of kin. But if you do not wish to claim it, tell
me so, that I may be guided accordingly, for no one has a
prior claim to yours, and mine is next." He answered, "I will
put in my claim."

⁵Boaz continued, "Once you acquire the field from Naomi,
you must take also Ruth the Moabite, the widow of the late
heir, and raise up a family for the departed on his estate."
⁶The near relative replied, "I cannot exercise my claim lest I
depreciate my own estate. Put in a claim yourself in my
stead, for I cannot exercise my claim." ⁷Now it used to be the
custom in Israel that, to make binding a contract of redemption or exchange, one party would take off his sandal and
give it to the other. This was the form of attestation in Israel.
⁸So the near relative, in saying to Boaz, "Acquire it for yourself," drew off his sandal. ⁹Boaz then said to the elders and
to all the people, "You are witnesses today that I have acquired from Naomi all the holdings of Elimelech, Chilion
and Mahlon. ¹⁰I also take Ruth the Moabite, the widow of
Mahlon, as my wife, in order to raise up a family for her late
husband on his estate, so that the name of the departed may
not perish among his kinsmen and fellow citizens. Do you
witness this today?" ¹¹All those at the gate, including the
elders, said, "We do so. May the LORD make this wife come
into your house like Rachel and Leah, who between them
built up the house of Israel. May you do well in Ephrathah
and win fame in Bethlehem. ¹²With the offspring the LORD
will give you from this girl, may your house become like the
house of Perez, whom Tamar bore to Judah."

¹³Boaz took Ruth. When they came together as man and
wife, the LORD enabled her to conceive and she bore a son.
¹⁴Then the women said to Naomi, "Blessed is the LORD who
has not failed to provide you today with an heir! May he become famous in Israel! ¹⁵He will be your comfort and the
support of your old age, for his mother is the daughter-in-

law who loves you. She is worth more to you than seven sons!" [16]Naomi took the child, placed him on her lap, and became his nurse. [17]And the neighbor women gave him his name, at the news that a grandson had been born to Naomi. They called him Obed. He was the father of Jesse, the father of David.

[18]These are the descendants of Perez: Perez was the father of Hezron, [19]Hezron was the father of Ram, Ram was the father of Amminadab, [20]Amminadab was the father of Nahshon, Nahshon was the father of Salmon, [21]Salmon was the father of Boaz, Boaz was the father of Obed, [22]Obed was the father of Jesse, and Jesse became the father of David.

All ends happily in this short story. Boaz settles the prior claim and marries Ruth. The witnesses bless her in the names of three great women: "Rachel and Leah, who between them built up the house of Israel" and Tamar, who bore Perez to Judah. The blessing of the witnesses is fulfilled. As Rachel and Leah were the mothers of Israel's twelve tribes, Ruth becomes the great grandmother of David, Israel's greatest king. Like Tamar, Ruth is a foreign woman who acted unconventionally in order to fulfill the levirate obligation to her dead husband. Like Perez, Ruth's son Obed continues the line of the covenant people.

The neighbor women also praise Ruth. They rejoice with Naomi in the daughter-in-law who loves her: "She is worth more to you than seven sons." Seven is the number of fullness or completion. There can be no greater praise in a society where a woman's worth and survival were dependent on sons.

Ruth is a foreign woman, a Moabite, who not only practices covenant virtues but becomes a mother of the covenant people. The devoted love between Ruth and Naomi, two childless and powerless widows, gives rise to the line of David whose dynasty, God promises, will endure forever (2 Sam 7:16). In Matthew's genealogy, which identifies Jesus as Son of David, Ruth is listed as one of his female ancestors (Matt 1:5).

HANNAH AND PENINNAH: TWO WIVES

1 Samuel 1:1-8

[1]There was a certain man from Ramathaim, Elkanah by name, a Zuphite from the hill country of Ephraim. He was

the son of Jeroham, son of Elihu, son of Tohu, son of Zuph, an Ephraimite. 2He had two wives, one named Hannah, the other Peninnah; Peninnah had children, but Hannah was childless. 3This man regularly went on pilgrimage from his city to worship the LORD of hosts and to sacrifice to him at Shiloh, where the two sons of Eli, Hophni and Phinehas, were ministering as priests of the LORD. 4When the day came for Elkanah to offer sacrifice, he used to give a portion each to his wife Peninnah and to all her sons and daughters, 5but a double portion to Hannah because he loved her, though the LORD had made her barren. 6Her rival, to upset her, turned it into a constant reproach to her that the LORD had left her barren. 7This went on year after year; each time they made their pilgrimage to the sanctuary of the LORD, Peninnah would approach her, and Hannah would weep and refuse to eat. 8Her husband Elkanah used to ask her: "Hannah, why do you weep, and why do you refuse to eat? Why do you grieve? Am I not more to you than ten sons?"

At the beginning of 1 Samuel we have another story in which the lives of women are intertwined. Elkanah of Ramathaim has two wives, one fruitful and one barren. It comes as no surprise that the one he loves more is Hannah, the barren wife. (Compare with Jacob and his two wives.) The situation pits the two women against each other. Peninnah, the fruitful wife, taunts Hannah because God has made her barren. Elkanah, to console Hannah, pleads, "Am I not more to you than ten sons?"

Peninnah appears only in the opening scene of the story (1:1-8). She is usually ignored, being seen as only a foil to Hannah. She has the blessing of many children and the sorrow of being loved less. The attention of her husband is turned to his other wife. The attention of the biblical author is also focused on Hannah. We are left to wonder what happened to Peninnah after Hannah began to have children. Did she lose even the small claim she had on her husband?

Hannah suffers also. Her husband is *not* worth more to her than ten sons. She is afflicted with barrenness, a curse in a society where women's worth is measured by the number of their sons. It is God who has done this to her (1:5-6). Nothing will console her except God's gift of sons.

1 Samuel 1:9-19

9Hannah rose after one such meal at Shiloh, and presented herself before the LORD; at the time, Eli the priest was sitting on a chair near the doorpost of the LORD's temple. 10In her bitterness she prayed to the LORD, weeping copiously, 11and she made a vow, promising: "O LORD of hosts, if you look with pity on the misery of your handmaid, if you remember me and do not forget me, if you give your handmaid a male child, I will give him to the LORD for as long as he lives; neither wine nor liquor shall he drink, and no razor shall ever touch his head." 12As she remained long at prayer before the LORD, Eli watched her mouth, 13for Hannah was praying silently; though her lips were moving, her voice could not be heard. Eli, thinking her drunk, 14said to her, "How long will you make a drunken show of yourself? Sober up from your wine!" 15"It isn't that, my lord," Hannah answered. "I am an unhappy woman. I have had neither wine nor liquor; I was only pouring out my troubles to the LORD. 16Do not think your handmaid a ne'er-do-well; my prayer has been prompted by my deep sorrow and misery." 17Eli said, "Go in peace, and may the God of Israel grant you what you have asked of him." 18She replied, "Think kindly of your maid-servant," and left. She went to her quarters, ate and drank with her husband, and no longer appeared downcast. 19Early the next morning they worshiped before the LORD, and then returned to their home in Ramah.

Elkanah and his family regularly went to worship God at the shrine where the ark of the covenant was then housed. The ark of the covenant, probably constructed during the desert period, was Israel's sign of the abiding presence of God with the people. The ark, a wooden chest, was said to contain the tablets of the law, a jar of manna, and Aaron's staff which bloomed. Cherubim stood on each side as guardians; their outstretched wings over the ark formed the throne of God. During the time of the judges (ca. 1250-1000 B.C.E.) the ark traveled from shrine to shrine. At the time of this story the ark was at Shiloh.

On one of the family's regular pilgrimages Hannah went into the shrine to pray before the ark. She poured out her grief to God and asked for a son. She promised that if God answered her prayer she would dedicate this son to God as a perpetual nazirite.[2] Eli, the priest who served the ark, could not understand what Hannah was doing. She clearly was not offering a sacrifice, the common mode of worship. She was making no sound. Only her lips were moving. Eli concluded that she was drunk and scolded her for acting inappropriately in the presence of God. Hannah explained her grief to him and Eli blessed her. Hannah then left the sanctuary in peace.

In this story Hannah begins the tradition of private prayer. Hers is the first story of someone coming to a shrine, not for public worship or sacrifice, but simply to speak to God from the heart. She knows how to pour out her troubles to God and to remain in God's presence. She is not afraid to explain to the official religious representative what she is doing. He is persuaded by her words and his scolding ends in blessing. When she leaves the sanctuary Hannah's prayer is already answered; God has given peace to her heart.

1 Samuel 1:19-28

When Elkanah had relations with his wife Hannah, the LORD remembered her. [20]She conceived, and at the end of her term bore a son whom she called Samuel, since she had asked the LORD for him. [21]The next time her husband Elkanah was going up with the rest of his household to offer the customary sacrifice to the LORD and to fulfill his vows, [22]Hannah did not go, explaining to her husband, "Once the child is weaned, I will take him to appear before the LORD and to remain there forever; I will offer him as a perpetual nazirite." [23]Her husband Elkanah answered her: "Do what you think best; wait until you have weaned him. Only, may the LORD bring your resolve to fulfillment!" And so she remained at home and nursed her son until she had weaned him.

[24]Once he was weaned, she brought him up with her, along with a three-year-old bull, an ephah of flour, and a skin of wine, and presented him at the temple of the LORD in Shiloh. [25]After the boy's father had sacrificed the young bull, Hannah, his mother, approached Eli [26]and said: "Pardon,

[2]See the discussion of the nazirite vow in the commentary on Samson's mother.

my lord! As you live, my lord, I am the woman who stood
near you here, praying to the LORD. 27I prayed for this child,
and the LORD granted my request. 28Now I, in turn, give him
to the LORD; as long as he lives, he shall be dedicated to the
LORD." She left him there;

God remembers Hannah. Whenever God remembers,
something significant happens (cf. Gen 8:1; Exod 2:24). God
remembers and Hannah conceives a son. She names him
Samuel, and interprets the name to mean "asked of God."3 As
long as Samuel is nursing, Hannah does not go to the sanctuary but remains at home with her child. When he is weaned,
she takes Samuel to the sanctuary, along with a generous sacrifice to offer him to God. She not only dedicates him as a perpetual nazirite, she also leaves him in the service of the shrine
where the ark is located.

The fact that there is a story of Samuel's infancy indicates
that Hannah's son will play a significant role in Israel's salvation history. Just as Moses was instrumental in Israel's move
from slavery to freedom, so Samuel is instrumental in the
move from tribal leadership to unity under a king. He is the
last of the judges; he it is who anoints Israel's first two kings,
Saul and David. Both the story of Moses and the story of
Samuel begin with courageous and faith-filled women.

1 Samuel 2:1-10

1and as she worshiped the LORD, she said:

"My heart exults in the LORD,
    my horn is exalted in my God.
I have swallowed up my enemies;
    I rejoice in my victory.
2There is no Holy One like the LORD;
    there is no Rock like our God.

3"Speak boastfully no longer,
    nor let arrogance issue from your mouths.
For an all-knowing God is the LORD,
    a God who judges deeds.

3The name Samuel actually means "his name is God."

⁴The bows of the mighty are broken,
    while the tottering gird on strength.
⁵The well-fed hire themselves out for bread,
    while the hungry batten on spoil.
The barren wife bears seven sons,
    while the mother of many languishes.
⁶"The LORD puts to death and gives life;
    he casts down to the nether world;
    he raises up again.
⁷The LORD makes poor and makes rich,
    he humbles, he also exalts.
⁸He raises the needy from the dust;
    from the ash heap he lifts up the poor,
To seat them with nobles
    and make a glorious throne their heritage.
He gives to the vower his vow,
    and blesses the sleep of the just.

"For the pillars of the earth are the LORD's,
    and he has set the world upon them.
⁹He will guard the footsteps of his faithful ones,
    but the wicked shall perish in the darkness.
For not by strength does man prevail;
¹⁰ the LORD's foes shall be shattered.
The Most High in heaven thunders;
    the LORD judges the ends of the earth,
Now may he give strength to his king,
    and exalt the horn of his anointed!"

When Hannah dedicates her son to God, she sings a hymn. Thus she joins Miriam and Deborah as the voice of Israel's praise. Many of the phrases of the song echo the psalms. The primary theme is God's preference for the poor and powerless. Hannah stands in a long tradition of the ʿanawim, the humble people whose total reliance is on God.

God has granted Hannah her heart's desire; there is no god like Israel's God (2:1-2). The Lord humbles those who rely on their own power: the mighty, the well-fed, the fertile wife. The Lord exalts those who know their only hope is in God: the tottering, the hungry, the barren wife (2:3-5). All power belongs to God; God uses this power in favor of the lowly (2:6-8). The final stanza of the song restates the theme: It is God who has power; the power of human beings comes not from their own strength but from God (2:8-10). The final verse, which mentions the king, the anointed (messiah), is an anticipation of the work of Hannah's son in making kings.

The song of Hannah is the model for Mary's song in Luke 1:46-55. Mary, herself one of the ʿanawim, is the virgin who bears a son, not through human power but through the power and mercy of God.

1 Samuel 2:11-21

11When Elkanah returned home to Ramah, the child remained in the service of the LORD under the priest Eli.

12Now the sons of Eli were wicked; they had respect neither for the LORD 13nor for the priests' duties toward the people. When someone offered a sacrifice, the priest's servant would come with a three-pronged fork, while the meat was still boiling, 14and would thrust it into the basin, kettle, caldron, or pot. Whatever the fork brought up, the priest would keep. That is how all the Israelites were treated who came to the sanctuary at Shiloh. 15In fact, even before the fat was burned, the priest's servant would come and say to the man offering the sacrifice, "Give me some meat to roast for the priest. He will not accept boiled meat from you, only raw meat." 16And if the man protested to him, "Let the fat be burned first as is the custom, then take whatever you wish," he would reply, "No, give it to me now, or else I will take it by force." 17Thus the young men sinned grievously in the presence of the LORD; they treated the offerings to the LORD with disdain.

18Meanwhile the boy Samuel, girt with a linen apron, was serving in the presence of the LORD. 19His mother used to make a little garment for him, which she would bring him each time she went up with her husband to offer the customary sacrifice. 20And Eli would bless Elkanah and his wife, as they were leaving for home. He would say, "May the LORD repay you with children from this woman for the gift she has made to the LORD!" 21The LORD favored Hannah so that she conceived and gave birth to three more sons and two daughters, while young Samuel grew up in the service of the LORD.

In the midst of a comparison which favors Samuel over Eli's sons, Hannah appears for a last time. The regular pilgrimage of Elkanah's family to the sanctuary is mentioned again. Hannah, however, no longer appears as the grieving wife but as the tender mother who brings her little son new clothes every time she comes. Eli remembers Hannah with blessing and God favors her. She gives birth to five more children, three sons and two daughters. The last verse of Psalm 113 can well be applied to Hannah: God "gives the childless wife a home, / the joyful mother of children."

6. Women of Israel's Monarchy

Suggested Readings: 1 Samuel 18:20–19:17; 2 Samuel 3:6-30; 6:1-23; 11:1–12:25; 13:1-22; 1 Kings 1:1–2:25; 10:1-13; 16:29-33; 18–19; 21; 2 Kings 9.

MICHAL

THE BRIDE

1 Samuel 18:20-29

20Now Saul's daughter Michal loved David, and it was reported to Saul, who was pleased at this, 21for he thought, "I will offer her to him to become a snare for him, so that the Philistines may strike him." [Thus for the second time Saul said to David, "You shall become my son-in-law today."] 22Saul then ordered his servants to speak to David privately and to say: "The king is fond of you, and all his officers love you. You should become the king's son-in-law." 23But when Saul's servants mentioned this to David, he said: "Do you think it easy to become the king's son-in-law? I am poor and insignificant." 24When his servants reported to him the nature of David's answer, 25Saul commanded them to say this to David: "The king desires no other price for the bride than the foreskins of one hundred Philistines, that he may thus take vengeance on his enemies." Saul intended in this way to bring about David's death through the Philistines. 26When the servants reported this offer to David, he was pleased with the prospect of becoming the king's son-in-law. [Before the year was up,] 27David made preparations and sallied forth with his men and slew two hundred Philistines. He brought back their foreskins and counted them out before the king, that he might thus become the king's son-in-law. So Saul gave him his daughter Michal in marriage. 28Saul thus came to recognize that the LORD was with David;

besides, his own daughter Michal loved David. ²⁹Therefore Saul feared David all the more [and was his enemy ever after].

Saul, Israel's first king, had three sons and two daughters. The younger daughter is named Michal (1 Sam 14:49). Michal's story is framed by two sentences: "Saul's daughter Michal loved David" (1 Sam 18:20); "Saul's daughter Michal . . . despised [David] in her heart" (2 Sam 6:16). Throughout her story she is used as a pawn by men seeking power.

In the beginning Michal loves David. Saul, seeing this, decides to use her to eliminate David. He offers her to David at the bride-price of one hundred Philistine foreskins. David must kill one hundred enemy men and return the evidence to the king. Saul is in hopes that the Philistines will kill David. Instead, David returns to Saul with evidence that he has killed two hundred Philistines. Saul's ploy does not work. Michal is given to David in marriage. She loves him; nowhere does the text tell us if he loves her.

1 Samuel 19:11-17

¹¹The same night, Saul sent messengers to David's house to guard it, that he might kill him in the morning. David's wife Michal informed him, "Unless you save yourself tonight, tomorrow you will be killed." ¹²Then Michal let David down through a window, and he made his escape in safety. ¹³Michal took the household idol and laid it in the bed, putting a net of goat's hair at its head and covering it with a spread. ¹⁴When Saul sent messengers to arrest David, she said, "He is sick." ¹⁵Saul, however, sent the messengers back to see David and commanded them, "Bring him up to me in the bed, that I may kill him." ¹⁶But when the messengers entered, they found the household idol in the bed, with the net of goat's hair at its head. ¹⁷Saul therefore asked Michal: "Why did you play this trick on me? You have helped my enemy to get away!" Michal answered Saul: "He threatened me, 'Let me go or I will kill you.'"

Saul continues his attempts to get rid of David. Possibly on the wedding night itself, Saul's soldiers surround David's house in order to kill him in the morning. But Michal protects

David. She helps him escape through a window and then puts the household idol, apparently a sizeable statue, into the bed so that the guards will suppose that it is David. When the trick is discovered, Saul accuses Michal of preferring David to him, her father. She makes the excuse that David threatened her. It is evident that her love for David is primary in her life. Her love for David protects him from her father Saul.

ONE OF DAVID'S WIVES

2 Samuel 3:12-16

> [12]Then Abner sent messengers to David in Telam, where he was at the moment, to say, "Make an agreement with me, and I will aid you by bringing all Israel over to you." [13]He replied, "Very well, I will make an agreement with you. But one thing I require of you. You must not appear before me unless you bring back Michal, Saul's daughter, when you come to present yourself to me." [14]At the same time David sent messengers to Ishbaal, son of Saul, to say, "Give me my wife Michal, whom I espoused by paying a hundred Philistine foreskins." [15]Ishbaal sent for her and took her away from her husband Paltiel, son of Laish, [16]who followed her weeping as far as Bahurim. But Abner said to him, "Go back!" And he turned back.

When David fled from Saul (1 Sam 21:1), he did not take Michal with him. Subsequently he married Abigail, Ahinoam (1 Sam 25:39-43), Maacah, Haggith, Shephatiah, and Eglah (2 Sam 3:2-5). "But Saul gave David's wife Michal, Saul's own daughter, to Palti, son of Laish, who was from Gallim" (1 Sam 25:43).

After the death of Saul, David rules over Judah and Saul's son Ishbaal rules over Israel, which consists of the other tribes (2 Sam 2:1-11). Ishbaal's power resides in his army general Abner. Abner, however, quarrels with Ishbaal over one of Saul's concubines, so Abner decides to switch allegiances and come to David (2 Sam 3:6-11). David agrees to welcome Abner but insists that the price of his acceptance is the return of Michal to him as a wife. So Michal is taken away from Paltiel, who follows her for some distance weeping; and she is added to David's growing harem.

Michal is again the pawn of men in power. In getting her back, David gains the possibility of uniting his dynasty with the house of Saul, thus gaining a double claim to rule over the twelve tribes. David and his descendants have a claim because of David's anointing as king (1 Samuel 16); Saul's descendants (through Michal) have a claim because of the anointing of Saul (1 Samuel 10). David also demonstrates his strength; Ishbaal is forced to send his sister to his rival king. No consideration is taken of the feelings of Michal, who must have been greatly loved by her second husband. Who can guess how she feels as she returns to be one of David's many wives?

2 Samuel 6:16-23

16As the ark of the LORD was entering the City of David, Saul's daughter Michal looked down through the window and saw King David leaping and dancing before the LORD, and she despised him in her heart. 17The ark of the LORD was brought in and set in its place within the tent David had pitched for it. Then David offered holocausts and peace offerings before the LORD. 18When he finished making these offerings, he blessed the people in the name of the LORD of hosts. 19He then distributed among all the people, to each man and each woman in the entire multitude of Israel, a loaf of bread, a cut of roast meat, and a raisin cake. With this, all the people left for their homes.

20When David returned to bless his own family, Saul's daughter Michal came out to meet him and said, "How the king of Israel has honored himself today, exposing himself to the view of the slave girls of his followers, as a commoner might do!" 21But David replied to Michal: "I was dancing before the LORD. As the LORD lives, who preferred me to your father and his whole family when he appointed me commander of the LORD's people, Israel, not only will I make merry before the LORD, 22but I will demean myself even more. I will be lowly in your esteem, but in the esteem of the slave girls you spoke of I will be honored." 23And so Saul's daughter Michal was childless to the day of her death.

The crisis comes as David reaches the peak of his power. He has conquered Jerusalem and made it his capital. Now he brings the ark of the covenant, sign of God's presence, to his city so that Jerusalem might become the city of God. As David dances in celebration, Michal watches him with hatred in her heart. She accosts him when he returns to the palace, scorning his public demonstration. In a scathing retort he reminds her that God has preferred the house of David to the house of her father Saul. Whatever love that may have remained between these two members of rival royal families is now dead as is the dream of uniting the two dynasties. Michal is doomed to seclusion in the harem for the rest of her life. David will never send for her. "So Saul's daughter Michal was childless to the day of her death."

Michal's story is a tragedy. The man she loved and whose life she saved uses her only as a claim to power. In the struggle she is taken from the only man who truly loved her. She is a sacrifice to the claims of Israel's monarchy.

BATHSHEBA

WIFE OF URIAH

2 Samuel 11:1-5

1At the turn of the year, when kings go out on campaign, David sent out Joab along with his officers and the army of Israel, and they ravaged the Ammonites and besieged Rabbah. David, however, remained in Jerusalem. 2One evening David rose from his siesta and strolled about on the roof of the palace. From the roof he saw a woman bathing, who was very beautiful. 3David had inquiries made about the woman and was told, "She is Bathsheba, daughter of Eliam, and wife of [Joab's armor-bearer] Uriah the Hittite." 4Then David sent messengers and took her. When she came to him, he had relations with her, at a time when she was just purified after her monthly period. She then returned to her house. 5But the woman had conceived, and sent the information to David, "I am with child."

Bathsheba is a beautiful woman, the wife of one of David's soldiers. When David sees her from his roof, he desires her. He sends for her, takes her, and sends her home. There is no word of love or affection, but only lust, power, and self-gratification.

When Bathsheba realizes that she has conceived, she speaks the one word recorded of her in Second Samuel: "I am pregnant." We are not told who bears the responsibility in this incident: Bathsheba, who was bathing in the privacy of her home but someplace where the king could see her, or David, the king who sends for her and impregnates her. It would seem that David is more accountable. A woman and a foreigner may have little choice when the messengers of the king come for her.

2 Samuel 11:6-17

6David therefore sent a message to Joab, "Send me Uriah the Hittite." So Joab sent Uriah to David. 7When he came, David questioned him about Joab, the soldiers, and how the war was going, and Uriah answered that all was well. 8David then said to Uriah, "Go down to your house and bathe your feet." Uriah left the palace, and a portion was sent out after him from the king's table. 9But Uriah slept at the entrance of the royal palace with the other officers of his lord, and did not go down to his own house. 10David was told that Uriah had not gone home. So he said to Uriah, "Have you not come from a journey? Why, then, did you not go down to your house?" 11Uriah answered David, "The ark and Israel and Judah are lodged in tents, and my lord Joab and your majesty's servants are encamped in the open field. Can I go home to eat and to drink and to sleep with my wife? As the LORD lives and as you live, I will do no such thing." 12Then David said to Uriah, "Stay here today also, I shall dismiss you tomorrow." So Uriah remained in Jerusalem that day. On the day following, 13David summoned him, and he ate and drank with David, who made him drunk. But in the evening he went out to sleep on his bed among his lord's servants, and did not go down to his home. 14The next morning David wrote a letter to Joab which he sent by Uriah. 15In it he directed: "Place Uriah up front, where the fighting is fierce. Then pull back and leave him to be struck down dead." 16So while Joab was besieging the city, he assigned Uriah to a place where he knew the defenders were strong. 17When the men of the city made a sortie against Joab, some officers of David's army fell, and among them Uriah the Hittite died.

When David learns that Bathsheba is pregnant, he uses all his resources to cover up his action. It is interesting to note that a woman and her pregnancy can make the king so desperate. First he sends for her husband, in the hope that Uriah will sleep with his wife. But Uriah, out of respect for the other soldiers in the field, will not go home. The second night David gets him drunk, hoping that he will go to Bathsheba, but again Uriah spends the night in the barracks. So David determines that Uriah must die. Uriah carries his own death warrant to the commander, an order from David that Uriah be abandoned at the front lines. Bathsheba's husband is to be killed in order to protect the honor of the king. David shows no concern for Bathsheba herself. Her loss will be grave. Her husband Uriah is a noble soldier, single-hearted in his devotion to duty and loyalty to the king. David, father of the child she carries, is intent only on covering his guilt, even to the point of murder.

2 Samuel 11:18-25

18Then Joab sent David a report of all the details of the battle, 19instructing the messenger, "When you have finished giving the king all the details of the battle, 20the king may become angry and say to you: 'Why did you go near the city to fight? Did you not know that they would shoot from the wall above? 21Who killed Abimelech, son of Jerubbaal? Was it not a woman who threw a millstone down on him from the wall above, so that he died in Thebez? Why did you go near the wall?' Then you in turn shall say, 'Your servant Uriah the Hittite is also dead.'" 22The messenger set out, and on his arrival he relayed to David all the details as Joab had instructed him. 23He told David: "The men had us at a disadvantage and came out into the open against us, but we pushed them back to the entrance of the city gate. 24Then the archers shot at your servants from the wall above, and some of the king's servants died, among them your servant Uriah." 25David said to the messenger: "This is what you shall convey to Joab: 'Do not be chagrined at this, for the sword devours now here and now there. Strengthen your attack on the city and destroy it.' Encourage him."

Joab carries out David's orders and sends a message to the king that Uriah is dead. Included in the message is a reference to Abimilech, the king of Shechem who was killed when a woman threw a millstone down on his head. The obvious connection is to the questionable strategy of placing troops too close to the city wall. Joab may also be expressing his opinion that, just as a woman killed Abimilech, a woman (Bathsheba) killed Uriah. Or that this incident will be as deadly for David, the king, as the incident at Thebez was deadly for another king, Abimilech.

WIFE OF DAVID

2 Samuel 11:26-27

> 26When the wife of Uriah heard that her husband had died, she mourned her lord. 27But once the mourning was over, David sent for her and brought her into his house. She became his wife and bore him a son. But the LORD was displeased with what David had done.

Bathsheba mourns for her dead husband and then is brought to the palace to join the other wives of David. There is no indication as to whether she goes willingly or not. There is also no description of the depth of her grief. Her choice and preference are not mentioned throughout the story. In due time the child of the king is born to her.

"The LORD was displeased with what David had done." David has committed adultery, arranged for the husband's murder, and taken the widow as his wife. There is no mention of God's anger with Bathsheba and no judgment expressed that Bathsheba has sinned.

2 Samuel 12:1-12

> 1The LORD sent Nathan to David, and when he came to him, he said: "Judge this case for me! In a certain town there were two men, one rich, the other poor. 2The rich man had flocks and herds in great numbers. 3But the poor man had nothing at all except one little ewe lamb that he had bought. He nourished her, and she grew up with him and his children. She shared the little food he had and drank from his cup and slept in his bosom. She was like a daughter to him. 4Now, the rich man received a visitor, but he would not take from his own flocks and herds to prepare a meal for the wayfarer who had

come to him. Instead he took the poor man's ewe lamb and made a meal of it for his visitor." [5]David grew very angry with that man and said to Nathan: "As the LORD lives, the man who has done this merits death! [6]He shall restore the ewe lamb fourfold because he has done this and has had no pity."

[7]Then Nathan said to David: "You are the man! Thus says the LORD God of Israel: 'I anointed you king of Israel. I rescued you from the hand of Saul. [8]I gave you your lord's house and your lord's wives for your own. I gave you the house of Israel and of Judah. And if this were not enough, I could count up for you still more. [9]Why have you spurned the LORD and done evil in his sight? You have cut down Uriah the Hittite with the sword; you took his wife as your own, and him you killed with the sword of the Ammonites. [10]Now, therefore, the sword shall never depart from your house, because you have despised me and have taken the wife of Uriah to be your wife.' [11]Thus says the LORD: 'I will bring evil upon you out of your own house. I will take your wives while you live to see it, and will give them to your neighbor. He shall lie with your wives in broad daylight. [12]You have done this deed in secret, but I will bring it about in the presence of all Israel, and with the sun looking down.'"

David's court prophet Nathan uses a parable to lead the king to pass judgment on himself: "The man who has done this merits death!" Nathan's parable convicts David as the guilty party, the one who took another man's wife. Bathsheba is portrayed as a little ewe lamb, helpless as she is stolen from one man to feed the appetite of another. The parable indicates that in the encounter she has died. Certainly her life has been irrevocably changed.

David's sin will lead to suffering for his other wives and for many innocent members of his family throughout future generations. His child will die. His daughter Tamar will be raped and cast aside (2 Sam 13:1-22). His sons will be killed (2 Sam 13:28-29; 18:14-15). His wives will be shamed and handed over to others (2 Sam 16:21-22).

2 Samuel 12:13-25

[13]Then David said to Nathan, "I have sinned against the LORD." Nathan answered David: "The LORD on his part has

forgiven your sin: you shall not die. [14]But since you have utterly spurned the LORD by this deed, the child born to you must surely die." [15]Then Nathan returned to his house.

The LORD struck the child that the wife of Uriah had borne to David, and it became desperately ill. [16]David besought God for the child. He kept a fast, retiring for the night to lie on the ground clothed in sackcloth. [17]The elders of his house stood beside him urging him to rise from the ground; but he would not, nor would he take food with them. [18]On the seventh day, the child died. David's servants, however, were afraid to tell him that the child was dead, for they said: "When the child was alive, we spoke to him, but he would not listen to what we said. How can we tell him the child is dead? He may do some harm!" [19]But David noticed his servants whispering among themselves and realized that the child was dead. He asked his servants, "Is the child dead?" They replied, "Yes, he is." [20]Rising from the ground, David washed and anointed himself, and changed his clothes. Then he went to the house of the LORD and worshiped. He returned to his own house, where at his request food was set before him, and he ate. [21]His servants said to him: "What is this you are doing? While the child was living, you fasted and wept and kept vigil; now that the child is dead, you rise and take food." [22]He replied: "While the child was living, I fasted and wept, thinking, 'Perhaps the LORD will grant me the child's life.' [23]But now he is dead. Why should I fast? Can I bring him back again? I shall go to him, but he will not return to me." [24]Then David comforted his wife Bathsheba. He went and slept with her; and she conceived and bore him a son, who was named Solomon. The LORD loved him [25]and sent the prophet Nathan to name him Jedidiah, on behalf of the LORD.

David repents of his sin: adultery and murder. The guilt may be David's but the punishment falls on Bathsheba as well: her son will die. The royal house to which she has come will be filled with violence. The narrator describes David's grief; Bathsheba's grief is only hinted at in the mention of David's comfort. (This is the only time that David expresses concern for Bathsheba's feelings.) She conceives a second son by this man who has brought her so much sorrow. This second son, Solomon, is beloved by the Lord, a gift of God's grace.

Bathsheba's future is now dependent on the fate of her son. She disappears from the story until he grows to manhood.

MOTHER OF SOLOMON

1 Kings 1:11-34

[11]Then Nathan said to Bathsheba, Solomon's mother: "Have you not heard that Adonijah, son of Haggith, has become king without the knowledge of our lord David? [12]Come now, let me advise you so that you may save your life and that of your son Solomon. [13]Go, visit King David, and say to him, 'Did you not, lord king, swear to your handmaid: Your son Solomon shall be king after me and shall sit upon my throne? Why, then, has Adonijah become king?' [14]And while you are still there speaking to the king, I will come in after you and confirm what you have said."

[15]So Bathsheba visited the king in his room, while Abishag the Shunamite was attending him because of his advanced age. [16]Bathsheba bowed in homage to the king, who said to her, "What do you wish?" [17]She answered him: "My lord, you swore to me your handmaid by the LORD, your God, that my son Solomon should reign after you and sit upon your throne. [18]But now Adonijah has become king, and you, my lord king, do not know it. [19]He has slaughtered oxen, fatlings, and sheep in great numbers; he has invited all the king's sons, Abiathar the priest, and Joab, the general of the army, but not your servant Solomon. [20]Now, my lord king, all Israel is waiting for you to make known to them who is to sit on the throne after your royal majesty. [21]If this is not done, when my lord the king sleeps with his fathers, I and my son Solomon will be considered criminals."

[22]While she was still speaking to the king, the prophet Nathan came in. [23]When he had been announced, the prophet entered the king's presence and, bowing to the floor, did him homage. [24]Then Nathan said: "Have you decided, my lord king, that Adonijah is to reign after you and sit on your throne? [25]He went down today and slaughtered oxen, fatlings, and sheep in great numbers; he invited all the king's sons, the commanders of the army, and Abiathar the priest, and they are eating and drinking in his company and saying, 'Long live King Adonijah!' [26]But me, your servant, he did not invite; nor Zadok the priest, nor Benaiah, son of

Jehoiada, nor your servant Solomon. ²⁷Was this done by my royal master's order without my being told who was to succeed to your majesty's kingly throne?"

²⁸King David answered, "Call Bathsheba here." When she re-entered the king's presence and stood before him, ²⁹the king swore, "As the LORD lives, who has delivered me from all distress, ³⁰this very day I will fulfill the oath I swore to you by the LORD, the God of Israel, that your son Solomon should reign after me and should sit upon my throne in my place." ³¹Bowing to the floor in homage to the king, Bathsheba said, "May my lord, King David, live forever!" ³²Then King David summoned Zadok the priest, Nathan the prophet, and Benaiah, son of Jehoiada. When they had entered the king's presence, ³³he said to them: "Take with you the royal attendants. Mount my son Solomon upon my own mule and escort him down to Gihon. ³⁴There Zadok the priest and Nathan the prophet are to anoint him king of Israel, and you shall blow the horn and cry, 'Long live King Solomon!'"

Bathsheba reappears at the critical moment when the successor to David must be decided. Two of David's sons have been eliminated from the choice: Amnon and Absalom are dead. Adonijah is now planning to be the next king. The crisis brings Bathsheba and Nathan together again. Nathan concocts a plot. First Bathsheba will suggest to the elderly king that he had promised that her son Solomon would succeed him on the throne. Then Nathan will come in and remind the king of the same promise. It is unclear whether David actually made this promise or not. It is possible that the promise is simply Nathan's invention. The conniving of Nathan and Bathsheba is successful. David orders the anointing of Solomon as king.

In proposing the plot Nathan says to Bathsheba, "Come now, let me advise you so that you may save your life and that of your son Solomon." His suggestion is a reminder that the life of rival heirs to the throne and the life of their mothers is in danger. Nathan appeals to Bathsheba's fear and sense of survival. Once more Bathsheba's future is dependent on the will of the king and the fate of her son.

In this scene Bathsheba shows herself a woman of power in contrast to two other women, Abishag and Haggith. Abishag is present when Bathsheba enters. She is a passive character throughout the story, having been brought to the king to attend him, to nurse him, and to keep him warm. But she is not a sexual partner of the king (1 Kings 1:2-4); she is not the mother of any of his sons. She never speaks; she exercises no power. Haggith is the mother of David's son, Adonijah. She too is wronged by David. She loses her son in the struggle for the throne (1 Kings 2:23-25). We do not know what becomes of her. It is the son of Bathsheba whom "the Lord loved" (2 Sam 12:24) who succeeds his father David.

1 Kings 2:12-25

12When Solomon was seated on the throne of his father David, with his sovereignty firmly established, 13Adonijah, son of Haggith, went to Bathsheba, the mother of Solomon. "Do you come as a friend?" she asked. "Yes," he answered, 14and added, "I have something to say to you." She replied, "Say it." 15So he said: "You know that the kingdom was mine, and all Israel expected me to be king. But the kingdom escaped me and became my brother's, for the LORD gave it to him. 16But now there is one favor I would ask of you. Do not refuse me." And she said, "Speak on." 17He said, "Please ask King Solomon, who will not refuse you, to give me Abishag the Shunamite for my wife." 18"Very well," replied Bathsheba, "I will speak to the king for you."

19Then Bathsheba went to King Solomon to speak to him for Adonijah, and the king stood up to meet her and paid her homage. Then he sat down upon his throne, and a throne was provided for the king's mother, who sat at his right. 20"There is one small favor I would ask of you," she said. "Do not refuse me." "Ask it, my mother," the king said to her, "for I will not refuse you." 21So she said, "Let Abishag the Shunamite be given to your brother Adonijah for his wife." 22"And why do you ask Abishag the Shunamite for Adonijah?" King Solomon answered his mother. "Ask the kingdom for him as well, for he is my elder brother and has with him Abiathar the priest and Joab, son of Zeruiah." 23And King Solomon swore by the LORD: "May God do thus and so to me, and more besides, if Adonijah has not proposed this at the cost of his life. 24And now, as the LORD lives, who has seated me firmly on the throne of my father David and made of me a dynasty as he promised, this day

shall Adonijah be put to death." [25]Then King Solomon sent
Benaiah, son of Jehoiada, who struck him dead.

The fate of rivals for the throne is demonstrated in the
story of Adonijah. He comes to enlist Bathsheba's aid in ac-
quiring David's last concubine. She does as Adonijah asks.
The story is not as innocent as it seems, however. Possession
of the king's concubines demonstrates the power of the
throne. When Absalom revolted against David, his taking of
the king's concubines in public view was a claim to the king's
power (2 Sam 16:21-22). Solomon sees the request for Abishag
as a threat and orders the death of Adonijah.

Once more Bathsheba's motives are not revealed. Does she
ask in innocence as a favor to Adonijah? Or is her action a
subtle way of removing a threat to her son's rule and her own
security? The narrator leaves us to wonder.

Bathsheba's position in Solomon's court is noteworthy.
She who entered David's court in shame receives Solomon's
homage as she approaches. A throne is provided for her at
the king's right. She is the first biblical "queen mother." In
Judah (the southern kingdom) the queen mother seems to
have held a position of influence. Fifteen of the passages list-
ing the succession of a king to the throne also name his
mother (1 Kings 15:2; 22:42; 2 Kings 8:26; 12:2; 14:2; 15:2, 33;
18:2; 21:1, 19; 22:1; 23:31, 36; 24:8, 18). There are additional
comments about some of these women. King Asa of Judah
"deposed his grandmother Maacah from her position as queen
mother," because she had participated in the worship of
Asherah (1 Kings 15:13; cf. 14:21). The queen mother Athaliah
reigns over Judah for six years (2 Kings 11:3). The mother of
King Jehoiachin of Judah is specifically named as one of the
significant exiles in the first deportation to Babylon (2 Kings
24:12, 15; Jer 29:2).[1] In the northern kingdom (Israel) Jezebel
is called "queen mother" (2 Kings 10:13) and seems to have
continued to wield influence during the reign of her son Joram
(2 Kings 9:22).

---

[1]Each of these women, like Bathsheba, is the mother of a younger son
who succeeds to the throne rather than an elder brother (or uncle).

MEMORY OF BATHSHEBA

Bathsheba is mentioned only three more times in the Bible. In 1 Chronicles she appears as the mother of four of David's sons (1 Chron 3:5), but the story of David's adultery and murder of her husband is omitted by the Chronicler. The title of Psalm 51 indicates that the psalm is to be prayed in the voice of David "when Nathan the prophet came to him after his affair with Bathsheba" (Ps 51:2). She is one of the five women mentioned in Matthew's genealogy of Jesus: "David became the father of Solomon, whose mother had been the wife of Uriah" (Matt 1:6).

The story of Bathsheba remains a mystery. Her first husband is killed by her second. Her first son dies as a punishment to the king; her second son succeeds him. She is of major significance in God's fulfillment of the promise to David that one of his sons will sit upon his throne (2 Samuel 7). Her son Solomon builds the Temple, acquires great wealth and a reputation for wisdom, and rules over Israel's largest empire. But Bathsheba's own motivations, intentions, and desires are never revealed. She is seen only through the stories of the powerful men who surround her.

TAMAR

A SISTER DESIRED

2 Samuel 13:1-6

[1]Some time later the following incident occurred. David's son Absalom had a beautiful sister named Tamar, and David's son Amnon loved her. [2]He was in such straits over his sister Tamar that he became sick; since she was a virgin, Amnon thought it impossible to carry out his designs toward her. [3]Now Amnon had a friend named Jonadab, son of David's brother Shimeah, who was very clever. [4]He asked him, "Prince, why are you so dejected morning after morning? Why not tell me?" So Amnon said to him, "I am in love with Tamar, my brother Absalom's sister." [5]Then Jonadab replied, "Lie down on your bed and pretend to be sick. When your father comes to visit you, say to him, 'Please let my sister Tamar come and encourage me to take food. If she prepares something appetizing in my presence, for me to

see, I will eat it from her hand.'" ⁶So Amnon lay down and pretended to be sick. When the king came to visit him, Amnon said to the king, "Please let my sister Tamar come and prepare some fried cakes before my eyes, that I may take nourishment from her hand."

In the story of Tamar, the structure of the first sentence illustrates her situation. She is a sister caught between two brothers. The two brothers are each named "David's sons," but Tamar is never identified as "David's daughter" although she is. Each brother has his own claim on her; after the disaster her father never claims her.

We also learn in the first paragraph that Tamar is beautiful and that she is a virgin. These good qualities will lead to her destruction. Her half-brother Amnon is so infatuated with her beauty that he makes himself sick. Since she is a virgin and thus valuable to the king as a possible wife for a foreign prince, Amnon knows he cannot have her. His friends encourage him to set up a situation in which he can be alone with Tamar. Then he can do to her whatever he wishes.

2 Samuel 13:7-13

⁷David then sent home a message to Tamar, "Please go to the house of your brother Amnon and prepare some nourishment for him." ⁸Tamar went to the house of her brother Amnon, who was in bed. Taking dough and kneading it, she twisted it into cakes before his eyes and fried the cakes. ⁹Then she took the pan and set out the cakes before him. But Amnon would not eat; he said, "Have everyone leave me." When they had all left him, ¹⁰Amnon said to Tamar, "Bring the nourishment into the bedroom, that I may have it from your hand." So Tamar picked up the cakes she had prepared and brought them to her brother Amnon in the bedroom. ¹¹But when she brought them to him to eat, he seized her and said to her, "Come! Lie with me, my sister!" ¹²But she answered him, "No, my brother! Do not shame me! That is an intolerable crime in Israel. Do not commit this insensate deed. ¹³Where would I take my shame? And you would be a discredited man in Israel. So please, speak to the king; he will not keep me from you."

David falls for the plot and sends Tamar to Amnon. She prepares the food and presents it to him, but he will not eat. He insists on being fed—alone—at her hand. When everyone else has left, he attempts first to seduce her.[2] He is his father's son, seeking sexual intimacy with a woman without regard for her desires. Tamar makes a counter-offer, suggesting that the king might give her to Amnon as a wife. She has a strong sense of her own honor and self-preservation. She is willing to find a solution which will protect her and satisfy Amnon's lust.

A SISTER RAPED AND REJECTED

2 Samuel 13:14-22

[14]Not heeding her plea, he overpowered her; he shamed her and had relations with her. [15]Then Amnon conceived an intense hatred for her, which far surpassed the love he had had for her. "Get up and leave," he said to her. [16]She replied, "No, brother, because to drive me out would be far worse than the first injury you have done me." He would not listen to her, [17]but called the youth who was his attendant and said, "Put her outside, away from me, and bar the door after her." [18]Now she had on a long tunic, for that is how maiden princesses dressed in olden days. When his attendant put her out and barred the door after her, [19]Tamar put ashes on her head and tore the long tunic in which she was clothed. Then, putting her hands to her head, she went away crying loudly. [20]Her brother Absalom said to her: "Has your brother Amnon been with you? Be still now, my sister; he is your brother. Do not take this affair to heart." But Tamar remained grief-stricken and forlorn in the house of her brother Absalom. [21]King David, who got word of the whole affair, became very angry. He did not, however, spark the resentment of his son Amnon, whom he favored because he was his first-born. [22]Absalom, moreover, said nothing at all to Amnon, although he hated him for having shamed his sister Tamar.

Amnon refuses to listen to Tamar. He wants her now. He rapes her and then he hates her. In spite of her pleas he throws

[2]The verb "to lie with" is a euphemism in Hebrew for sexual intercourse.

her out of the house and locks the door. Weeping, she tears the garment that signified her virginal status. She goes to her full brother Absalom who conceives a terrible hatred for Amnon. David, however, does nothing because he does not want to offend his first-born son.

The occurrences of the family words "brother," "sister," "son," reveal the irony of Tamar's tragedy. Although Tamar's "family" relationship to Amnon and to David is repeatedly mentioned, the relationship is distorted and ignored by both men. In verse 1 the *sister* is caught between the two *sons*. Amnon is in distress over his *sister* (13:2) and tells his friend that he is in love with his *brother's sister* (13:4). His friend advises him to ask his *father* to send his *sister* (13:5). So Amnon asks the king to send his *sister* and David sends her to her *brother* (13:6-7). Tamar goes to the house of her *brother* (13:8), bakes cakes and brings them to her *brother* (13:10). Instead he says, "Lie with me, my *sister*" (13:11), but she refuses, "No, my *brother*" (13:12). After he has raped her and wants to drive her out, she protests, "No, *brother*" (13:16). She flees to her *brother* Absalom who says, "Has your *brother* Amnon been with you? Be still now, my *sister*; he is your *brother*." "But she remained grief-stricken and forlorn in the house of her *brother*" (13:20). David did not want to offend his *son* (13:21) but Absalom hated Amnon for raping his *sister* (13:22). The word "sister" occurs eight times, "brother" ten times, "son" three times," "father" once.

Memory of Tamar

In spite of the abundance of references to family relationships, Tamar is never called David's daughter. As a daughter she is insignificant and even expendable. It is sons who are important in this search for the next king. The word "daughter" does not even occur in the passage. Its next appearance is in a reference to Absalom's children: "Absalom had three sons born to him, besides a daughter named Tamar, who was a beautiful woman" (14:27). This daughter is undoubtedly named for Absalom's sister, perhaps in grief, perhaps as a way to honor Tamar.

Tamar's tragedy is part of David's punishment for his
adultery with Bathsheba and the murder of her husband. It
is part of the violence that Nathan predicted would never
depart from the house of David. The tragedy also has a direct
effect on the succession. Amnon was the supposed heir to
the throne, but in revenge for his rape of Tamar, Absalom
murders him (2 Sam 13:23-33). Then Absalom, another possible heir, flees (2 Sam 13:34-38). Even when he returns, he is
never fully reconciled to the king (2 Sam 14:28-33). Eventually he mounts a revolt and drives David from Jerusalem
(2 Sam 15:1-18). The revolt is put down and Absalom is killed
(2 Sam 18:1-18), thus removing another heir to the throne.
Throughout the story David grieves over his sons (2 Sam
13:39; 18:12; 19:1-5). There is never a word of grief over his
daughter.

QUEEN OF SHEBA

1 Kings 10:1-13

¹The queen of Sheba, having heard of Solomon's fame, came
to test him with subtle questions. ²She arrived in Jerusalem
with a very numerous retinue, and with camels bearing
spices, a large amount of gold, and precious stones. She
came to Solomon and questioned him on every subject in
which she was interested. ³King Solomon explained everything she asked about, and there remained nothing hidden
from him that he could not explain to her.

⁴When the queen of Sheba witnessed Solomon's great wisdom, the palace he had built, ⁵the food at his table, the seat-
ing of his ministers, the attendance and garb of his waiters,
his banquet service, and the holocausts he offered in the
temple of the LORD, she was breathless. ⁶"The report I heard
in my country about your deeds and your wisdom is true,"
she told the king. ⁷"Though I did not believe the report until
I came and saw with my own eyes, I have discovered that
they were not telling me the half. Your wisdom and prosperity surpass the report I heard. ⁸Happy are your men,
happy these servants of yours, who stand before you always
and listen to your wisdom. ⁹Blessed be the LORD, your God,
whom it has pleased to place you on the throne of Israel. In
his enduring love for Israel, the LORD has made you king to

carry out judgment and justice." [10]Then she gave the king one hundred and twenty gold talents, a very large quantity of spices, and precious stones. Never again did anyone bring such an abundance of spices as the queen of Sheba gave to King Solomon.

[11]Hiram's fleet, which used to bring gold from Ophir, also brought from there a large quantity of cabinet wood and precious stones. [12]With the wood the king made supports for the temple of the LORD and for the palace of the king, and harps and lyres for the chanters. No more such wood was brought or seen to the present day.

[13]King Solomon gave the queen of Sheba everything she desired and asked for, besides such presents as were given her from Solomon's royal bounty. Then she returned with her servants to her own country.

Sheba (or Seba) is probably a tribe of northwest Arabia. Sheba is listed as a caravan people by Job (Job 6:19) and the Sabeans carry off Job's farm animals in the prologue (Job 1:15; cf. Joel 4:8). They are traders of incense (Jer 6:20), precious stones, gold, and textiles (Ezek 27:22-24). The wealth of Seba/Sheba is indicated in several places: "the kings of Arabia and Seba offer gifts" (Ps 72:10; cf Isa 60:6).

Even though Sheba is generally agreed to be an Arabian tribe, there is a contrasting tradition that locates Sheba with the Ethiopians. Gen 10:7 lists Seba as one of the descendants of Cush (Ethiopia). Josephus, a first-century Jewish historian, also assumes the queen comes from Ethiopia. There is a tradition in Ethiopia that the kings are descended from Solomon and the Queen of Sheba. This royal line, called the "Lion of Judah," remained in power in Ethiopia until 1974.

According to the biblical story the queen of Sheba comes to Solomon to test his wisdom. In fact, she probably came to him to confirm trading agreements since trade was an important part of the Solomonic program (cf. 1 Kings 9:26-28; 10:14-29). The queen arrives with "camels bearing spices, a large amount of gold, and precious stones" (10:2). Before she leaves, she gives the king a great abundance of treasures (10:10). Solomon also gives her presents (10:13). The trading agreement seems to have been sealed.

Wisdom, however, is also an important part of Solomon's character. "He was wiser than all other [people] . . . and his fame spread throughout the neighboring nations. . . . [People] came to hear Solomon's wisdom from all nations, sent by all the kings of the earth who had heard of his wisdom" (1 Kings 5:11, 14). The queen is also wise; she has come to test Solomon with subtle questions (10:1). But Solomon is greater than she imagined; she is overwhelmed by his wisdom. She recognizes that Solomon's wisdom is a gift of God, a sign of God's love for Israel (10:9). She is impressed by Solomon's wealth and the culture of his court, added signs of his wisdom.

The queen of Sheba is an important witness to the wealth and wisdom of Solomon. She also gives praise to the Lord, Israel's God. Jesus recalls her openness to learn from Solomon in contrast to the hardness of heart of his contemporaries: "At the judgment the queen of the south will arise with this generation and condemn it, because she came from the ends of the earth to hear the wisdom of Solomon; and there is something greater than Solomon here" (Matt 12:42; cf. Luke 11:31).

JEZEBEL

QUEEN OF ISRAEL

1 Kings 16:29-33

29In the thirty-eighth year of Asa, king of Judah, Ahab, son of Omri, became king of Israel; he reigned over Israel in Samaria for twenty-two years. 30Ahab, son of Omri, did evil in the sight of the LORD more than any of his predecessors. 31It was not enough for him to imitate the sins of Jeroboam, son of Nebat. He even married Jezebel, daughter of Ethbaal, king of the Sidonians, and went over to the veneration and worship of Baal. 32Ahab erected an altar to Baal in the temple of Baal which he built in Samaria, 33and also made a sacred pole. He did more to anger the LORD, the God of Israel, than any of the kings of Israel before him.

Jezebel is the daughter of Ethbaal, the king of the Phoenicians,[3] and the wife of Ahab, king of Israel. Ahab belongs to

---

[3]The Phoenicians are here called the Sidonians for one of their primary cities, Sidon.

the dynasty of Omri, one of the most prosperous of Israel's dynasties. Other peoples of the Ancient Near East continued to call Israel "the house of Omri" long after the dynasty had disappeared.

Phoenicia is located on the Mediterranean coast north of Israel. Two of its major cities were Tyre and Sidon. These Phoenician ports prospered through the production of purple goods and the shipping trade. The Phoenicians, like the Canaanites, worshiped the god Baal. When Jezebel came to Israel she brought with her prophets of Baal and encouraged worship of him. Ahab, like Solomon before him, built a shrine for the worship of his wife's god (cf. 1 Kings 11:4-10).

The biblical stories of the kings of Israel (the northern kingdom) are told by writers from Judah (the southern kingdom).[4] Thus these kings and queens are presented in a negative light and are often judged solely on the basis of their devotion to the Jerusalem temple and the worship decreed as proper by the Jerusalem priests.

RIVAL OF ELIJAH

1 Kings 18:3-4

[3]Now the famine in Samaria was bitter, [4]and Ahab had summoned Obadiah, his vizier, who was a zealous follower of the LORD. When Jezebel was murdering the prophets of the LORD, Obadiah took a hundred prophets, hid them away fifty each in two caves, and supplied them with food and drink.

1 Kings 19:1-3

[1]Ahab told Jezebel all that Elijah had done—that he had put all the prophets to the sword. [2]Jezebel then sent a messenger to Elijah and said, "May the gods do thus and so to me if by this time tomorrow I have not done with your life what was done to each of them." [3]Elijah was afraid and fled for his life, going to Beer-sheba of Judah.

---

[4]After the death of Solomon (922 B.C.E.) the kingdom divided, with Solomon's son Rehoboam becoming king of Judah (and the tribe of Benjamin, which was absorbed into the tribe of Judah) and Jeroboam son of Nebat becoming king of Israel (the other ten tribes).

Jezebel and the prophet Elijah become mortal enemies. Each sees the other's unflinching devotion to a god as a deadly threat. Jezebel murders the prophets of Yahweh; Elijah, in a mocking contest, murders the prophets of Baal (1 Kings 18). Jezebel, exercising her royal authority, condemns Elijah to death and he flees.

The names of the two express their bitter opposition. In the Septuagint (or Greek) version, Jezebel says to Elijah: "If you are Elijah, I am Jezebel" (19:2). The name "Elijah" means "Yahweh is my God." The name "Jezebel" probably means "The Prince [Baal] is mine." Jezebel and Elijah are a matched pair, each single-mindedly committed to his or her god.

MURDER OF NABOTH

1 Kings 21:1-26

¹Some time after this, as Naboth the Jezreelite had a vineyard in Jezreel next to the palace of Ahab, king of Samaria, ²Ahab said to Naboth, "Give me your vineyard to be my vegetable garden, since it is close by, next to my house. I will give you a better vineyard in exchange, or, if you prefer, I will give you its value in money." ³"The LORD forbid," Naboth answered him, "that I should give you my ancestral heritage." ⁴Ahab went home disturbed and angry at the answer Naboth the Jezreelite had made to him: "I will not give you my ancestral heritage." Lying down on his bed, he turned away from food and would not eat.

⁵His wife Jezebel came to him and said to him, "Why are you so angry that you will not eat?" ⁶He answered her, "Because I spoke to Naboth the Jezreelite and said to him, 'Sell me your vineyard, or, if you prefer, I will give you a vineyard in exchange.' But he refused to let me have his vineyard." ⁷"A fine ruler over Israel you are indeed!" his wife Jezebel said to him. "Get up. Eat and be cheerful. I will obtain the vineyard of Naboth the Jezreelite for you."

⁸So she wrote letters in Ahab's name and, having sealed them with his seal, sent them to the elders and to the nobles who lived in the same city with Naboth. ⁹This is what she wrote in the letters: "Proclaim a fast and set Naboth at the head of the people. ¹⁰Next, get two scoundrels to face him and accuse him of having cursed God and king. Then take

him out and stone him to death." [11]His fellow citizens—the elders and the nobles who dwelt in his city—did as Jezebel had ordered them in writing, through the letters she had sent them. [12]They proclaimed a fast and placed Naboth at the head of the people. [13]Two scoundrels came in and confronted him with the accusation, "Naboth has cursed God and king." And they led him out of the city and stoned him to death. [14]Then they sent the information to Jezebel that Naboth had been stoned to death.

[15]When Jezebel learned that Naboth had been stoned to death, she said to Ahab, "Go on, take possession of the vineyard of Naboth the Jezreelite which he refused to sell you, because Naboth is not alive, but dead." [16]On hearing that Naboth was dead, Ahab started off on his way down to the vineyard of Naboth the Jezreelite, to take possession of it.

[17]But the LORD said to Elijah the Tishbite: [18]"Start down to meet Ahab, king of Israel, who rules in Samaria. He will be in the vineyard of Naboth, of which he has come to take possession. [19]This is what you shall tell him, 'The LORD says: After murdering, do you also take possession? For this, the Lord says: In the place where the dogs licked up the blood of Naboth, the dogs shall lick up your blood, too.'" [20]"Have you found me out, my enemy?" Ahab said to Elijah. "Yes," he answered. "Because you have given yourself up to doing evil in the LORD's sight, [21]I am bringing evil upon you: I will destroy you and will cut off every male in Ahab's line, whether slave or freeman, in Israel. [22]I will make your house like that of Jeroboam, son of Nebat, and like that of Baasha, son of Ahijah, because of how you have provoked me by leading Israel into sin." [23](Against Jezebel, too, the LORD declared, "The dogs shall devour Jezebel in the district of Jezreel.") [24]"When one of Ahab's line dies in the city, dogs will devour him; when one of them dies in the field, the birds of the sky will devour him." [25]Indeed, no one gave himself up to the doing of evil in the sight of the LORD as did Ahab, urged on by his wife Jezebel. [26]He became completely abominable by following idols, just as the Amorites had done, whom the LORD drove out before the Israelites.

In the story of Naboth's vineyard, Jezebel appears ruthless. She does not understand the importance of land to the Israelite. She does not know the significance of land as a sign of participation in the covenant. Thus she cannot understand Naboth's insistence on keeping his little vineyard. Why will he not sell or trade it? Neither does she understand the relationship between the king and the law in Israel. She does not see that the king, too, is subject to the law of Israel, which is the law of God. Thus she does not understand the hesitation of her husband. Why does he not simply exercise his royal power and seize the vineyard?

If Ahab will not act as king, she will act as queen. She takes matters into her own hands. As David had arranged the death of Uriah, Jezebel arranges the death of Naboth. According to Israelite law, a man could be condemned if the testimony of two witnesses agreed. Jezebel commands the people to produce two accusers and Naboth is executed. Then Jezebel returns to her husband to announce that it is possible for him to take possession of the coveted vineyard.

On the way to the vineyard Ahab encounters Jezebel's mortal enemy, Elijah. Elijah announces the doom of the house of Ahab because of the murder of Naboth. The doom centers on Ahab; Jezebel is mentioned only parenthetically. Ahab will be punished because he listened to her; she, too, will die a horrible death. Because he responds to Elijah's announcement with humility and repentance, Ahab himself is spared (1 Kings 21:27-29). Nothing more is said here of Jezebel's fate.

DEATH OF JEZEBEL

2 Kings 9:30-37

> 30When Jezebel learned that Jehu had arrived in Jezreel, she shadowed her eyes, adorned her hair, and looked down from her window. 31As Jehu came through the gate, she cried out, "Is all well, Zimri, murderer of your master?" 32Jehu looked up to the window and shouted, "Who is on my side? Anyone?" At this, two or three eunuchs looked down toward him. 33"Throw her down," he ordered. They threw her down, and some of her blood spurted against the wall and against the horses. Jehu rode in over her body 34and, after eating and drinking, he said: "Attend to that accursed woman and bury her; after all, she was a king's daughter." 35But when they went to bury her, they found nothing of her but the skull, the feet, and the hands. 36They

returned to Jehu, and when they told him, he said, "This is the sentence which the LORD pronounced through his servant Elijah the Tishbite: 'In the confines of Jezreel dogs shall eat the flesh of Jezebel. ³⁷The corpse of Jezebel shall be like dung in the field in the confines of Jezreel, so that no one can say: This was Jezebel.'"

The death of Jezebel represents the final encounter between Jezebel and Elijah. When Elijah fled from Jezebel's anger, he went to Mount Sinai (Horeb). There God spoke to him in "a tiny whispering sound" (1 Kings 19:12). God commissioned Elijah to raise three people to power: Elisha as prophet after him, Hazael as king of Syria, Jehu as king of Israel. Elijah appoints Elisha who carries out the other two parts of the commission. When Elisha anoints Jehu as king, Jehu gathers an army and kills the kings of both Israel and Judah along with most of the royal families (2 Kings 9). Among those killed are seventy of Ahab's descendants, thus fulfilling Elijah's prophecy against the house of Ahab (2 Kings 10:1-11). Ahab himself is already dead.

Jehu also sets out against Jezebel. She dresses herself as befits a queen in order to meet her adversary. She addresses him as Zimri, who had assassinated Elah, king of Israel, a little more than thirty years before. Zimri himself ruled only seven days and killed himself during the attack by Omri, Jezebel's father-in-law (1 Kings 16:9-15). Royal to the last, she scorns Jehu and predicts that his reign will be short, a prediction that did not come to pass.

Jezebel is thrown to the ground by her servants and dies. But when Jehu decides to give her a burial fitting a king's daughter, he is too late. As Elijah had prophesied, the dogs have eaten her flesh. "No one can say: This was Jezebel." Elijah has won.

MEMORY OF JEZEBEL

Jezebel has become a symbol for the worst that can be said about women. Because she puts on her makeup and dresses in her royal finery to meet Jehu, she has been identified as a whore (cf. Rev 2:20). There is no indication in the text that this identification is true. When Jehu accuses her of fornication and witchcraft (9:22), it is probably a reference to her worship of Baal. She is also considered to be a power-hungry woman who will eliminate anyone who stands in her way. Her treatment of Naboth would confirm this. It must be remembered, however, that she is exercising royal prerogative similar to that of other kings and queens of the Ancient Near East, including David and Solomon. Their example does not excuse her action but rather gives it perspective. Finally, she and Elijah clash over the most important theological question of the ninth century (and other centuries as well): Who is God in Israel? Elijah is victorious in the struggle; Yahweh is God in Israel.

7. Woman, Image of God

Suggested Readings: Genesis 1–3; Proverbs 8–9; 31:10-31; Sirach 1; 24; 51; Wisdom 7–9

The women portrayed in the preceding chapters are figures in Israel's history from the time of Abraham (ca. 1800 B.C.E.) to the time of the kings (tenth to sixth century B.C.E.) In the tenth century, the time of David and Solomon, Israel began to consider wider issues. How did the world come to be? Where did the other nations come from? What could be said about human nature? Who is Man? Who is Woman? What could be said about the nature of God? How can one describe the relationship between God and human beings? The opening chapters of the Book of Genesis represent Israel's reflection on these questions.

Israel's wise men deepened this reflection on human nature and the nature of God. They described the bridge uniting God and human beings as Wisdom. The image they used for God's Wisdom is the image of woman. The portrayal of the Wisdom Woman is found in the Books of Proverbs, Sirach (Ecclesiasticus), and the Wisdom of Solomon.

THE GENESIS IDEAL

CREATION

Genesis 1:26-31

26Then God said: "Let us make man in our image, after our likeness. Let them have dominion over the fish of the sea, the birds of the air, and the cattle, and over all the wild animals and all the creatures that crawl on the ground."

27God created man in his image;
  in the divine image he created him;
  male and female he created them.

28God blessed them, saying: "Be fertile and multiply; fill the earth and subdue it. Have dominion over the fish of the sea, the birds of the air, and all the living things that move on the earth." 29God also said: "See, I give you every seed-bearing plant all over the earth and every tree that has seed-bearing fruit on it to be your food; 30and to all the animals of the land, all the birds of the air, and all the living creatures that crawl on the ground, I give all the green plants for food." And so it happened. 31God looked at everything he had made, and he found it very good. Evening came, and morning followed—the sixth day.

The story of creation which opens the Book of Genesis is a major theological work. Genesis 1 was written by the final editor around the sixth century as an introduction to the whole Pentateuch (Genesis–Deuteronomy). It presents an image of God, a description of all other reality known to the author, and the relationship of God to this great world and its inhabitants. God is powerful and commanding, creating everything by a word. First God creates space and time—day and night, sky and earth, land and sea (Gen 1:3-10)—and then all those things which exist within space and time (Gen 1:11-31). Then God rests. All things are in order: each in its proper place, each in proper relationship to the other. Everything that God has created is good.

As the culmination of this creative activity, God makes human beings. "Then God said: 'Let us make *ʾadam* in our image, after our likeness'" (1:26). The Hebrew word *ʾadam* is the generic term meaning "human" or "humanity." God creates all humanity and every human being in the divine image and likeness. Male and female are created by God in the divine image (1:27).

Because human beings are in God's image, they share God's life and power. This sharing of divine life is what blessing means. God gives them authority and responsibility over all other creation (1:26, 28). They become the channel through which God's lifegiving love comes to every other creature.

God also gives them the power through their sexuality to continue creation (1:28). God entrusts them with the care and continuance of all that exists.

The theology of Genesis 1 portrays human beings—man and woman—as living images of God, representatives of and witnesses to God's power and love toward all creation. Women as well as men bear this responsibility and share this greatness. Women as well as men are made in the image of God. Women as well as men bring God's touch to the world and its inhabitants. The Israelites were forbidden to make any images of God (Exod 20:4). They already had images of God in their lives: each other. St. Irenaeus, a second-century theologian, said that "the glory of God is the human being fully alive." Women and men are the vision of God's glory on the face of the earth.

EVE

CREATION AGAIN

Genesis 2:21-24

²¹So the LORD God cast a deep sleep on the man, and while he was asleep, he took out one of his ribs and closed up its place with flesh. ²²The LORD God then built up into a woman the rib that he had taken from the man. When he brought her to the man, ²³the man said:

> "This one, at last, is bone of my bones
>   and flesh of my flesh;
> This one shall be called 'woman,'
>   for out of 'her man' this one has been taken."

²⁴That is why a man leaves his father and mother and clings to his wife, and the two of them become one body.

Gen 2:4b-25 is a second, older story of creation. It was written around the tenth century B.C.E. The first story (Gen 1:1–2:4a) describes God's creation of the whole world. This second story focuses on the creation and nature of human beings. The rest of creation is mentioned only secondarily as it relates to humans.

This creation story begins with the creation of the ʾadam. The Lord God forms the human creature, ʾadam, out of the clay

of the ground, the *ʾadamah*. The word, *ʾadam*, gives no indication of gender for this human creature throughout the chapter—the planting of the garden, the command not to eat of the
tree, the creation of the animals—until God's second creative
act in the formation of human beings.

The Lord God casts a deep sleep on the *ʾadam*, divides its
flesh, and creates sexuality (2:21-22). The first gender-specific
term for a human being appears in 2:22:[1] "The LORD God then
built up into a woman (*ʾishshah*) the rib that he had taken from
the human (*ʾadam*)." The other human being created from this
one flesh does not recognize his identity as man (*ʾish*) until he
recognizes the other, the woman. The delight expressed by the
ʾadam at this recognition gives witness to the oneness of flesh
between the man and the woman:

> "This one, at last, is bone of my bones
>   and flesh of my flesh;
> This one shall be called 'woman,'
>   for out of 'her man' this one has been taken" (2:23).

The next verse states clearly: "That is why a man leaves his
father and mother and clings to his wife, and the two of them
become one body." Man and woman are created from one
flesh and long to return to their original unity.

Just as male and female are created together in the image
of God in Genesis 1, so in Genesis 2 man and woman are created together to help one another. It is not good for a human
(the *ʾadam*) to be alone. So God, in great wisdom, gives man
and woman to each other, created from the same flesh.

TROUBLE IN THE GARDEN

Genesis 3:1-7

[1]Now the serpent was the most cunning of all the animals
that the LORD God had made. The serpent asked the woman,
"Did God really tell you not to eat from any of the trees in
the garden?" [2]The woman answered the serpent: "We may

---

[1]In Gen 1:27 the distinction is expressed by the biological terms
"male" (*zakar*) and "female" (*neqebah*).

eat of the fruit of the trees in the garden; [3]it is only about the fruit of the tree in the middle of the garden that God said, "'You shall not eat it or even touch it, lest you die.'" [4]But the serpent said to the woman: "You certainly will not die! [5]No, God knows well that the moment you eat of it your eyes will be opened and you will be like gods who know what is good and what is bad." [6]The woman saw that the tree was good for food, pleasing to the eyes, and desirable for gaining wisdom. So she took some of its fruit and ate it; and she also gave some to her husband, who was with her, and he ate it . [7]Then the eyes of both of them were opened, and they realized that they were naked; so they sewed fig leaves together and made loincloths for themselves.

The idyllic situation in the garden, however, is not perfect. Man and woman have been forbidden to eat from the tree of the knowledge of good and bad. To eat from the tree is to know and experience both good and bad. The pair are protected from bad, but they are also ignorant of good. To begin to know good and bad is a way of describing the transition from infancy to the dawning awareness of childhood or from childhood to adulthood.[2] To know good and bad is to be wise.[3] To know good and bad is to be like God.

The serpent, cleverest of all the animals God made (Gen 2:25), points out this deficiency to the man and the woman. The two are together when the serpent speaks (Gen 3:6), although only the woman responds. The serpent attempts to drive a wedge between the humans and God by suggesting that God is keeping them from all the good things in the garden. The woman knows this is not true; it is only one tree which is forbidden them. She, however, suggests they may not even touch it.

[2]The phrase, "knowledge of good and bad," is used in other biblical passages to describe children. The children who will be allowed to enter the land of promise are described as those "who as yet do not know good from bad" (Deut 1:39). The child who is a sign for Ahaz will not yet know "to reject the bad and choose the good" before the threat to Ahaz' kingdom is gone (Isa 7:15-16).

[3]The wise woman of Tekoa says that David is like an angel of God, knowing good and bad (2 Sam 14:17).

The serpent then focuses on the forbidden tree, the tree of the knowledge of good and bad. The serpent, in a classic portrayal of temptation, speaks the truth but deceives by means of it. The serpent makes three points: (1) you will not die; (2) your eyes will be opened; (3) you will be like God (or gods—the Hebrew word is the same for both). *You will not die:* the implication in 2:17 is that death will follow immediately upon eating from the tree. It is true, the two do not die immediately, but death will eventually come to them. *Your eyes will be opened:* their eyes are opened to see first their own vulnerability, their nakedness (Gen 3:7), and then to see the ever-widening set of choices between good and bad. *You will be like God:* in knowing the difference between good and bad they are indeed like God (cf. 2 Sam 14:17). They glimpse part of what God knows, but in turning away from God they have turned away from their source of life. They have threatened their greatest good, the breath of God which is their life (cf. Gen 2:7); they have opened themselves to their worst possibility, death. God confirms the truth of the serpent's words: "Then the LORD God said: 'See! The man has become like one of us, knowing what is good and what is bad! Therefore, he must not be allowed to put out his hand to take fruit from the tree of life also, and thus eat of it and live forever'" (Gen 3:22).

Both the man and the woman are present to hear the serpent's words. Both make the choice. Both eat from the tree. Both are told by God that their share in God's life and power, their capacity for fruitfulness, is damaged. The woman will suffer in pregnancy and childbirth;[4] the man will suffer in bringing forth food from the earth. Both will have to labor as they participate in the process of creation.

---

[4]Most translations obscure the fact that there are three terms in 3:16: "hard work," "pregnancies," "bear children." The verse reads literally: "I will increase your hard work and your pregnancies; with labor shall you bear children." The term for "hard work" (*ʿissabon*) appears also in 3:18, addressed to the man: "With hard work you shall eat of it [the earth] all the days of your life." See the Latin Vulgate. See also Carol Meyers, *Discovering Eve: Ancient Israelite Women in Context* (New York: Oxford University, 1988).

The story of chapters two and three ends in ambiguity. The man names the woman Eve, a name that in Hebrew sounds like "life," because she is the mother of all the living (Gen 3:20). She has faced the choice between barren immortality or fruitful mortality. She has decided to risk death for the sake of bearing children.[5] Paradoxically, she thus becomes a sign of hope, a sign of life in the face of death. The Lord God takes pity on the pair and makes leather garments for them. But God also banishes them from the garden and bars the way to the tree of life.

Woman and man share the same flesh, breathe the same breath. Woman and man are both responsible for breaking the bond with God, for bringing into human life the knowledge of both good and bad. Woman and man will each suffer death. Together, woman and man continue the blessing, even with struggle, of perpetuating life in the world.

WISDOM (SOPHIA)

STREET PREACHER

Proverbs 8:1-3

<blockquote>
1Does not Wisdom call,
   and Understanding raise her voice?
2On the top of the heights along the road,
   at the crossroads she takes her stand;
3By the gates at the approaches of the city,
   in the entryways she cries aloud.
</blockquote>

In the first chapters of the Book of Proverbs, written by the book's final editor around the fifth century B.C.E., a female figure appears who is the personification of the wisdom of God. The Wisdom Woman appears first as a prophet, a street preacher. She cries out at street corners and at the place of business, the city gates (cf. Prov 1:20-21). She has a message for human beings. She

---

[5]It has been suggested that had the two humans remained in the garden they would have been immortal, but as a consequence would also have had no children. It is death that makes children necessary and, considering the limitations of space, even possible. Compare Gen 1:28 in which there is no assumption that humans are immortal and thus their fertility is recognized as a blessing and a share in God's creative power.

offers to pour out her spirit upon them (Prov 1:23). She promises instruction better than silver, and knowledge better than gold (8:10). She is the source and strength of all the good things human beings do (8:12-16) and the provider of all the good things they enjoy (8:17-21). Who is this Wisdom Woman?

GOD'S FIRSTBORN

Proverbs 8:22-31

22"The LORD begot me, the firstborn of his ways,
   the forerunner of his prodigies of long ago;
23From of old I was poured forth,
   at the first, before the earth.
24When there were no depths I was brought forth,
   when there were no fountains or springs of water;
25Before the mountains were settled into place,
   before the hills, I was brought forth;
26While as yet the earth and the fields were not made,
   nor the first clods of the world.

27"When he established the heavens I was there,
   when he marked out the vault over the face of the deep;
28When he made firm the skies above,
   when he fixed fast the foundations of the earth;
29When he set for the sea its limit,
   so that the waters should not transgress his command;
30Then was I beside him as his craftsman,
   and I was his delight day by day,
Playing before him all the while,
   31playing on the surface of his earth;
   and I found delight in the sons of men.

In Prov 8:22-31 Wisdom sings a hymn describing her origins and her relationship to God and to human beings. She is God's firstborn, begotten before creation, brought to birth before earth and sea. She was not only present when God created space and time and every creature, she was God's architect, the designer of God's creation.[6] Through her all things were created.

---

[6]The Hebrew word *'amon* can be translated either "artisan" or "darling child." In 8:30, Wisdom is either the designer of God's creation or the child playing before God.

The final verses of this section (8:30-31) capture the reason for her great worth. She is the bridge between God and human beings. Two key words illustrate this function: "delight" and "play." She is God's delight; she finds delight in human beings. She plays before God; she plays on the earth. She lives in both worlds: God's and humanity's. Her signature, the way she can be recognized, is in play and delight. Through these two characteristics she joins God with humankind. Because of this function, all good things come through her.

The chapter closes with her exhortation (8:32-36). Again she calls to people to listen to her. Three beatitudes describe those who heed:

> 33Happy the man who obeys me,
>   and happy those who keep my ways,
> 34Happy the man watching daily at my gates,
>   waiting at my doorposts.

Why are they happy? Because those who find Wisdom find life and God's favor. In contrast, those who "miss her" harm their lives. The word "miss" comes from the common Hebrew word for sin. To sin in Hebrew is literally "to miss the mark." To "miss" Wisdom is equivalent to sin which brings death. Those who hate Wisdom love death (8:35-36).

THE BANQUET

Proverbs 9:1-5

> 1Wisdom has built her house,
>   she has set up her seven columns;
> 2She has dressed her meat, mixed her wine,
>   yes, she has spread her table.
> 3She has sent out her maidens; she calls
>   from the heights out over the city:
> 4"Let whoever is simple turn in here;
>   to him who lacks understanding, I say,
> 5Come, eat of my food,
>   and drink of the wine I have mixed!"

The Wisdom Woman has called out to people. Now she prepares the banquet to which she invites them. She builds her house: the world. She sets up seven columns: the perfect number; her house will not fall. She prepares the meat, mixes the wine, sets the table, sends out the invitations. Everything is in readiness. This offer of food and drink is an offer to partake of Wisdom herself. We have a saying, "you are what you eat." Wisdom says, "Eat of me and you will have life" (9:6, 11).

In Prov 3:18 Wisdom is described as the tree of life. In Genesis 2–3 the tree of life is at the center of the garden. Those who eat of it will live forever (cf. Gen 3:22). After the man and the woman ate from the tree of the knowledge of good and bad, God set a guard on the way to the tree of life (Gen 3:24). Now Wisdom proclaims that she is that tree of life. The gift of life is offered again. This food is not prohibited for human beings. On the contrary, people are exhorted to come, eat and drink. Those who partake of Wisdom find life.

Another female figure, Folly, is described in the introductory section of Proverbs (chs. 1–9). In chapter nine she also invites the simple to come and eat at her house. She, too, calls from the city heights. Her invitation sounds deceptively like the invitation of Wisdom:

> 16"Let whoever is simple turn in here,
>   or who lacks understanding; for to him I say,
> 17Stolen water is sweet,
>   and bread gotten secretly is pleasing!"

But her food is not truth and discipline. She offers deceit and wanton pleasure. The consequence of eating at her table is not life but death: "In the depths of the nether world are her guests" (Prov 9:18). In contrast to the Wisdom Woman, Folly never appears again. She herself disappears into the nether world.

The introductory section of Proverbs (chs. 1–9) is bound off by an inclusion (the same phrase at beginning and end). "The fear of the LORD is the beginning of knowledge" (Prov 1:7); "the beginning of wisdom is the fear of the LORD" (Prov 9:10). Fear of the Lord is awe at the greatness of God and wonder that this great God loves and cares for us. Fear of the Lord is the realization that God is God and we are not. Fear of the Lord leads to wisdom; wisdom leads to knowledge of God. To know God is to love God. Love of God leads to greater awe, greater fear of the Lord, greater wisdom. "Fear of the Lord" becomes another name for Wisdom.

WISDOM AS WIFE

Proverbs 31:10-31

[10]When one finds a worthy wife,
   her value is far beyond pearls.
[11]Her husband, entrusting his heart to her,
   has an unfailing prize.
[12]She brings him good, and not evil,
   all the days of her life.
[13]She obtains wool and flax
   and makes cloth with skillful hands.
[14]Like merchant ships,
   she secures her provisions from afar.
[15]She rises while it is still night,
   and distributes food to her household.
[16]She picks out a field to purchase;
   out of her earnings she plants a vineyard.
[17]She is girt about with strength,
   and sturdy are her arms.
[18]She enjoys the success of her dealings;
   at night her lamp is undimmed.
[19]She puts her hands to the distaff,
   and her fingers ply the spindle.
[20]She reaches out her hands to the poor,
   and extends her arms to the needy.
[21]She fears not the snow for her household;
   all her charges are doubly clothed.
[22]She makes her own coverlets;
   fine linen and purple are her clothing.
[23]Her husband is prominent at the city gates
   as he sits with the elders of the land.
[24]She makes garments and sells them,
   and stocks the merchants with belts.
[25]She is clothed with strength and dignity,
   and she laughs at the days to come.
[26]She opens her mouth in wisdom,
   and on her tongue is kindly counsel.
[27]She watches the conduct of her household,
   and eats not her food in idleness.

²⁸Her children rise up and praise her;
  her husband, too, extols her:
²⁹"Many are the women of proven worth,
  but you have excelled them all."
³⁰Charm is deceptive and beauty fleeting;
  the woman who fears the LORD is to be praised.
³¹Give her a reward of her labors,
  and let her works praise her at the city gates.

The Book of Proverbs ends with an acrostic poem of 22 lines.[7] It is a poem in praise of the valiant woman, the woman who has the strength *(hayil)* of a military man or the resources *(hayil)* of the wealthy. The virtues of this woman are overwhelming. She spins; she weaves; she makes clothes. She buys fields; she sells garments; with her profit she plants a vineyard. She takes care, not only of her own household, but also of the poor and needy. She teaches wisdom. Her husband and children can do nothing but praise her.

Who is this woman who cares for everything and everyone? Is she not Wisdom? At the beginning of the Book of Proverbs the young man was counseled to seek Wisdom, to court her, to do anything he could to obtain her. At the end of the book is a description of the happiness of the one who has taken Wisdom into his house and who lives with her. This woman, whose name is "Fear of the Lord" (cf. 31:30), will bring him the delights of life through all his days.[8] Proverbs ends with the happiness of the one who finds Wisdom.

WORD OF GOD/BREATH OF GOD

The Book of Sirach is constructed on three great pillars, three hymns to Wisdom, chapters 1, 24, and 51:13-30.[9] Ben Sira

---

[7]In an acrostic (or alphabetic) poem each verse begins with the next letter of the Hebrew alphabet. Most acrostics are twenty-two lines corresponding to the twenty-two letters of the Hebrew alphabet.

[8]Verse 30 can be translated, "The woman, Fear of the Lord, is to be praised." See Thomas P. McCreesh, "Wisdom as Wife: Proverbs 31:10-31," *Revue Biblique* 92 (1985) 25–46.

[9]A Jerusalem sage, Ben Sira, wrote at the beginning of the second century B.C.E. The Book of Sirach was written in Hebrew and translated into

introduces his discussion of the Wisdom Woman by echoing Proverbs 8: Wisdom comes from God, was created by God. It is God who knows her and pours her forth upon the world (Sir 1:1-8 [10]). Then the sage sings a hymn to Wisdom as Fear of the Lord (Sir 1:9-18 [11-20]). Fear of the Lord is the beginning, the fullness, the garland, and the root of Wisdom. Fear of the Lord (i.e., Wisdom) brings all good things to those who live by her.

Chapter 24, like Proverbs 8, contains a hymn of self-praise sung by Wisdom in which she describes herself, her origins, her relationship to God, and the good things she does for human beings.

Sirach 24:1-27 [29]

¹Wisdom sings her own praises,
  before her own people she proclaims her glory;
²In the assembly of the Most High she opens her mouth,
  in the presence of his hosts she declares her worth:
³"From the mouth of the Most High I came forth,
  and mistlike covered the earth.
⁴In the highest heavens did I dwell,
  my throne on a pillar of cloud.
⁵The vault of heaven I compassed alone,
  through the deep abyss I wandered.
⁶Over waves of the sea, over all the land,
  over every people and nation I held sway.

Greek by Ben Sira's grandson. At the end of the first century C.E., when the Jewish community made a final decision on which books would be included in the Hebrew Bible, the Book of Sirach was not included. Christians however continued to use it in the Greek translation. At the time of the Reformation, Protestant Christians began using only the books included in the Hebrew Bible. Roman Catholic Christians continued using other books from the Greek Bible including the Book of Sirach. Thus this book, which is found in Roman Catholic translations, will not be found in Protestant translations or will be in a special section labeled Apocrypha or Deutero-Canonical books. Also, there are several numbering systems for chapter and verse in the Book of Sirach because of the complexity of its textual tradition. The verses indicated here are those of the *New American Bible* with the *New Revised Standard Version* indicated in brackets.

7Among all these I sought a resting place;
   in whose inheritance should I abide?

8"Then the Creator of all gave me his command,
   and he who formed me chose the spot for my tent,
Saying, 'In Jacob make your dwelling,
   in Israel your inheritance.'
9Before all ages, in the beginning, he created me,
   and through all ages I shall not cease to be.
10In the holy tent I ministered before him,
   and in Zion I fixed my abode.
11Thus in the chosen city he has given me rest,
   in Jerusalem is my domain.
12I have struck root among the glorious people,
   in the portion of the LORD, his heritage.

13"Like a cedar on Lebanon I am raised aloft,
   like a cypress on Mount Hermon,
14Like a palm tree in Engedi,
   like a rosebush in Jericho,
Like a fair olive tree in the field,
   like a plane tree growing beside the water.
15Like cinnamon, or fragrant balm, or precious myrrh,
   I give forth perfume;
Like galbanum and onycha and sweet spices,
   like the odor of incense in the holy place.
16I spread out my branches like a terebinth,
   my branches so bright and so graceful.
17I bud forth delights like the vine,
   my blossoms become fruit fair and rich.

18 [19]Come to me, all you that yearn for me,
   and be filled with my fruits;
19 [20]You will remember me as sweeter than honey,
   better to have than the honeycomb.
20 [21]He who eats of me will hunger still,
   he who drinks of me will thirst for more;
21 [22]He who obeys me will not be put to shame,
   he who serves me will never fail."

22 [23]All this is true of the book of the Most High's covenant,
   the law which Moses commanded us
   as an inheritance for the community of Jacob.
23 [25]It overflows, like the Pishon, with wisdom—
   like the Tigris in the days of the new fruits.

24 [26]It runs over, like the Euphrates, with understanding,
   like the Jordan at harvest time.
25 [27]It sparkles like the Nile with knowledge,
   like the Gihon at vintage time.
26 [28]The first man never finished comprehending wisdom,
   nor will the last succeed in fathoming her.
27 [29]For deeper than the sea are her thoughts;
   her counsels, than the great abyss.

Wisdom begins by describing her origins (Sir 24:3-7). She came from the mouth of the Most High. She is God's Word, God's Breath/Spirit. As the spirit/wind that hovered over the waters (Gen 1:2) and the mist/stream that covered the earth at the beginning (cf. Gen 2:6), she is present at creation. She is universal; she is everywhere. Still she seeks a place to live, a place to rest. Her place, chosen for her by God, is in Jerusalem with God's covenant people (24:8-12). There she pitches her tent; there she ministers before God in the holy tent, the temple. She is available to all people, but she lives with Israel.

The image of Wisdom as tree echoes Proverbs (Sir 24:12-17; cf. Prov 3:18). She strikes root among God's people. She is like every beautiful tree—cedar, cypress, palm, olive. She is found everywhere from the north to the south (Lebanon to Jericho), from mountains to desert (Mount Hermon to Engedi). She offers everything pleasant to smell, see, and taste—cedar, roses, cinnamon, grapes. She feeds all who long for her (24:18-21 [19-22]). Her food is sweeter than honey; her food is herself! All who eat of her will hunger still, who drink of her will thirst for more. One will never be able to get enough. What she offers is life. She concludes her song with a promise similar to Prov 8:35-36. Those who obey her will not be shamed; those who serve her will not fall short. The word here is again related to the common Hebrew word for sin, i.e., "to miss the mark."

Ben Sira breaks new ground with his next statement: "All this is true of the book of the Most High's covenant, the law which Moses commanded us as an inheritance for the community of Jacob" (24:22 [23]). Wisdom, this wonderful woman who is God's Word, God's Spirit, is the Torah. She lives in Israel. Where she is to be found is in the Book of the Law, the Sacred Scripture of God's people. She is God's revelation of

self, the word of God in human words. She is present to anyone who meditates upon this book.

Ben Sira then compares Wisdom to the water of life (Sir
24:23-27 [25-29]). He echoes Gen 2:10-14, the description of the
four rivers that water the whole earth. To the Genesis list of
Pishon, Gihon, Tigris, and Euphrates, he adds the other rivers
of Israel's experience: the Jordan and the Nile. As these rivers
give life to all creation, so Wisdom gives life. No human being,
from the original *ʾadam* to the last, will ever exhaust Wisdom's
gifts. She is deeper even than the sea, the abyss of primeval
chaos (Gen 1:2). She is God's gift to human beings who have
an infinite thirst for truth and love (cf. Sir 24:20 [21]).

Wisdom can never be totally comprehended by human beings, but Ben Sira does not consider her inaccessible. In a pro-
found description of the role of the teacher, Ben Sira describes
his own work. He digs a little channel from Wisdom's stream in
order to water his garden. But no teacher can measure the
power of Wisdom flowing out through teaching. The little channel becomes a river; the river becomes a sea. Every teacher
labors, not only for the present time, but for every generation to
come. Wisdom, who is found in reflection on common human
experience, is available to everyone. But the teacher has special
responsibility to keep Wisdom's river clear and flowing.

WISDOM AS BRIDE

Sirach 51:13-30

13When I was young and innocent,
  I sought wisdom.
14She came to me in her beauty,
  and until the end I will cultivate her.
15As the blossoms yielded to ripening grapes,
  the heart's joy,
My feet kept to the level path
  because from earliest youth I was familiar with her.
16In the short time I paid heed,
  I met with great instruction.
17Since in this way I have profited,
  I will give my teacher grateful praise.

18I became resolutely devoted to her—
  the good I persistently strove for.

[19]I burned with desire for her,
  never turning back.
I became preoccupied with her,
  never weary of extolling her.
My hand opened her gate
  and I came to know her secrets.
[20]For her I purified my hands;
  in cleanness I attained to her.
At first acquaintance with her, I gained understanding
  such that I will never forsake her.
[21]My whole being was stirred as I learned about her;
  therefore I have made her my prize possession.
[22]The LORD has granted me my lips as a reward,
  and my tongue will declare his praises.

[23]Come aside to me, you untutored,
  and take up lodging in the house of instruction;
[24]How long will you be deprived of wisdom's food,
  how long will you endure such bitter thirst?
[25]I open my mouth and speak of her:
  gain, at no cost, wisdom for yourselves.
[26]Submit your neck to her yoke,
  that your mind may accept her teaching.
For she is close to those who seek her,
  and the one who is in earnest finds her.
[27]See for yourselves! I have labored only a little,
  but have found much.
[28]Acquire but a little instruction;
  you will win silver and gold through her.
[29]Let your spirits rejoice in the mercy of God,
  and be not ashamed to give him praise.
[30]Work at your tasks in due season,
  and in his own time God will give you your reward.

The Book of Sirach ends with an acrostic poem, a song of rejoicing from one who has found Wisdom. This poem is a passionate love song. In the first half the author describes his own experience. He sought Wisdom as a young man. He pursued her with devotion. He courted her with burning desire. He cleansed his whole life for her. She came to him in beauty. She stirred the center of his being. She became the subject of his every thought, the goal of his whole life.

In the second half of the poem (51:23-30) Ben Sira makes an offer to other young men. (Formal education at that time was limited to men.) If they will come to his school, they, too, will gain what he has found. She will satisfy their hunger and thirst. She will bring them silver and gold. She is the gift of God.

IMAGE OF GOD

Wisdom 7:22–8:1

22Wisdom, the artificer of all, taught me.
For in her is a spirit
   intelligent, holy, unique,
Manifold, subtle, agile,
   clear, unstained, certain,
Not baneful, loving the good, keen,
   unhampered, beneficent, 23kindly,
Firm, secure, tranquil,
   all-powerful, all-seeing,
And pervading all spirits,
   though they be intelligent, pure and very subtle.
24For Wisdom is mobile beyond all motion,
   and she penetrates and pervades all things by reason of
   her purity.
25For she is an aura of the might of God
   and a pure effusion of the glory of the Almighty;
   therefore nought that is sullied enters into her.
26For she is the refulgence of eternal light,
   the spotless mirror of the power of God,
   the image of his goodness.
27And she, who is one, can do all things,
   and renews everything while herself perduring;
And passing into holy souls from age to age,
   she produces friends of God and prophets.
28For there is nought God loves, be it not
   one who dwells with Wisdom.
29For she is fairer than the sun
   and surpasses every constellation of the stars.
Compared to light, she takes precedence;
30 for that, indeed, night supplants,
   but wickedness prevails not over Wisdom.
8:1Indeed, she reaches from end to end mightily
   and governs all things well.

The description of the Wisdom Woman in The Wisdom of
Solomon is the most intense and dramatic in the Bible.[10] This
first-century sage writes in the persona of Solomon, king of
Israel in the tenth century B.C.E. In the passage 6:22–9:18 he describes Solomon's experience with the Wisdom Woman. After
an introduction (6:22-25) there are two passages of Solomon's
personal experience (7:1-22a; 8:2-21) which surround an ecsta-
tic description of Wisdom herself (7:22b–8:1). The section concludes with a prayer (9:1-18).

Solomon begins by promising to share everything he
knows about Wisdom (6:22-25). He acknowledges that he is
human like everyone else, born in the ordinary way (7:1-6).
But he prayed and pleaded for Wisdom, recognizing that her
value reduced everything else to dust (7:7-9). "All good things
together came to [him] in her company" (7:11). He rejoiced in
Wisdom, the mother of all that is good (7:12).[11] He promises to
share Wisdom freely with everyone and prays to speak well of
her (7:13-16). He credits Wisdom with giving him knowledge
of all the major areas of knowledge in Greek education: as-
tronomy, physics, zoology and botany, medicine (7:17-22a). All
these things he learned because Wisdom, the craftswoman
(technitis) of all, taught him (cf. Prov 8:30).

The description of Wisdom (7:22b–8:1) begins with twenty-
one characteristics of her spirit. Twenty-one is the product of
two perfect numbers, three and seven. Wisdom is perfection
multiplied by perfection. But that is not enough for her description. She is the motion of all that moves; she penetrates
everything that exists. She is better than light. She rules all
things. Most important in her description, however, is her relationship to God and her relationship to human beings.

[10]The Wisdom of Solomon was written in Greek by a sage in Alexan-
dria sometime in the mid-first century B.C.E. Like the Book of Sirach (see
above), the Wisdom of Solomon was not included in the Hebrew Bible.
Thus it is in the canon (list) of the Roman Catholic Bible but not of
Protestant Bibles.

[11]Here, in order to describe the Wisdom Woman, the gifted author of
the book coins a new word in Greek, *genetis,* meaning "creator," "beget-
ter," "mother." The masculine term was already current, but the feminine
appears here for the first time.

This description of Wisdom's relationship to God is clearer and more intense than either Proverbs or Sirach. She is a breath of God's power, the outpouring of God's glory. She is the shining of God's light. She is the perfect reflection of God's power and goodness. She can do all things. Who is this Wisdom Woman? Is it true that everything we can say of God we can say of her?

Her relationship to human beings is of great benefit to us. She fills the prophets with God's word. She is the one who makes us friends of God. God loves those who live with Wisdom. The advice to seek her is very good advice indeed.

Solomon's testimony to his own experience both precedes (7:1-22a) and follows (Wis 8:2-21) the description of Wisdom. Solomon is the wise young man who seeks Wisdom as a bride. She will teach him everything that he needs for a full life (Wis 8:2-8). She gives him not only joy and peace; it is for her sake that he will have immortality (Wis 8:9-16). The concept of immortality is grasped very late in the Old Testament period. The good news of immortality is most fully described in this first-century B.C.E. book. Here (Wis 8:13) the author proclaims that this gift of immortality comes from Wisdom. Wisdom herself is a gift of God. Therefore Solomon, who is set up as a model for all of us, seeks her with all his energy (Wis 8:17-21).

The section concludes with a beautiful prayer for the gift of Wisdom (Wis 9:1-18) which leads into a narration of Israel's history seen through the lens of Wisdom's power to save (Wis 10:1–19:22).

CONCLUSION

In the Wisdom books we find a personification of God's Wisdom as woman. She is beautiful and desirable. Young men (and we, too) are advised to seek her, to court her, to bring her to live with them. For her part, she is actively seeking lovers. She promises no less than life. The final chapters of Proverbs and Sirach present Wisdom as wife. The person who has succeeded in winning her as spouse is rewarded with all the goodness and delight that life can bring.

The Book of Wisdom clarifies what Proverbs and Sirach have suggested. The Wisdom Woman is an image of God. In speaking of her, we speak of God. Thus the Wisdom Woman is Scripture's most powerful confirmation of creation's truth: "God created humankind in his image, in the image of God he created them; male and female he created them" (Gen 1:27, NRSV). Man is an image of God; woman is an image of God. There is no superiority of one over the other as image. The two together are the best image of God in all of creation.

8. Women of Courage and Strength

Suggested Readings: Judith 8–16; Daniel 13.

JUDITH

THE SETTING

In the first eight chapters of the Book of Judith we learn of the distress of the people of a little Israelite town named Bethulia. In order to emphasize the magnitude of their danger, the author has lined up and joined together the greatest enemies of Israel throughout its history: the Assyrians, terrible conquerors who took captive the ten tribes of the northern kingdom in 722 B.C.E.; and Nebuchadnezzar, king of the Babylonians, who destroyed Jerusalem and exiled the people of the southern kingdom in 587 B.C.E. These two peoples symbolize the greatest possible threat to God's people. This book indicates that the danger Judith's people face is as great as the danger of both these powerful enemies combined.

The author of the Book of Judith has deliberately confused the historical characters. Nebuchadnezzar (actually king of the Babylonians) is portrayed as king of the Assyrians. In this story the Assyrian army, in the name of King Nebuchadnezzar and under the leadership of General Holofernes, has conquered the whole Ancient Near East except the little country of Judea. The Israelites seem easy prey for this great power.

But, by also confusing historical dates, the author gives us several clues that God's people are not so easily defeated. The year given in the story seems to apply to the Babylonian exile (587–539 B.C.E.), not the Assyrian captivity, which began in 722 B.C.E. The Book of Judith says that Nebuchadnezzar (identified as king of the Assyrians) began his terrible conquest of the world in the eighteenth year of his reign on the twenty-second day of the first month (Jdt 2:1). The eighteenth year of Nebuchadnezzar's actual reign (in Babylon) was 587 B.C.E., the year of Jerusalem's destruction and the beginning of the exile, the worst moment in Israel's history. The use of this date suggests that perhaps Nebuchadnezzar will indeed be successful.

But the author's setting of Nisan as the month when Nebuchadnezzar's conquest began is a symbol that Israel will not fall before this formidable enemy. The first month of the Jewish year is Nisan (March–April), the month of Passover which celebrates God's deliverance of the Israelites when they were most helpless, the greatest moment in Israel's history. The actual month of Nebuchadnezzar's conquest of Jerusalem and the beginning of the Babylonian exile was Av (close to our August).

But if we still miss the point that God will save them no matter how great the difficulty, the author gives us one more clue. Again dates are mixed up and yet another year is suggested. The book tells us that the people have just been saved by God again; they have just returned from exile (539 B.C.E.; Jdt 4:3). So even as chapter two suggests that this is 587, their worst moment, chapter four indicates that it is really 539, the moment of their deliverance. How can we doubt that God will continue to deliver them from their enemies?

This mixing of dates and years and countries may seem confusing to us, but the author is not intending to give us a historical portrayal. Rather the author is telling a story that is larger than life. Israel's greatest enemies and worst defeats are all rolled into one "mega-enemy." The most dramatic examples of God's salvation throughout their history are all rolled into one "mega-rescue." Why would an author do this? This author wants to encourage the people of the second century B.C.E. (the time when the book was written) to believe that God will again rescue them, that no enemy can defeat them if they cling to God. In the second century the people are threatened by King Antiochus of Syria. They fear for their lives and for the loss of their Jewish tradition. The story of Judith was written to strengthen the faith of these believers.

A HOLY WIDOW

Judith 8:1-8

¹Now in those days Judith, daughter of Merari, son of Joseph, son of Oziel, son of Elkiah, son of Ananias, son of Gideon, son of Raphain, son of Ahitob, son of Elijah, son of Hilkiah, son of Eliab, son of Nathanael, son of Salamiel, son of Sarasadai, son of Simeon, son of Israel, heard of this. ²Her husband, Manasseh, of her own tribe and clan, had died at the time of the barley harvest. ³While he was in the field supervising those who bound the sheaves, he suffered sunstroke; and he died of this illness in Bethulia, his native city. He was buried with his forefathers in the field between Dothan and Balamon. ⁴The widowed Judith remained three years and four months at home, ⁵where she set up a tent for herself on the roof of her house. She put sackcloth about her loins and wore widow's weeds. ⁶She fasted all the days of her widowhood, except sabbath eves and sabbaths, new moon eves and new moons, feastdays and holidays of the house of Israel. ⁷She was beautifully formed and lovely to behold. Her husband, Manasseh, had left her gold and silver, servants and maids, livestock and fields, which she was maintaining. ⁸No one had a bad word to say about her, for she was a very God-fearing woman.

It is a surprise to readers that, in the book that bears her name, Judith does not appear until chapter eight. The first seven chapters are devoted to the accomplishments and boasting of her chief adversary, Holofernes, Nebuchadnezzar's army general. Judith, whose name means "Jewess," is introduced with a sixteen-member genealogy that goes back to Israel/Jacob. The extensive genealogy is an indication of the importance of her story in the tradition of Israel. She is a widow and thus potentially helpless in Israelite society. However, she is also wealthy, due to the foresight of her dead husband. Finally, she is a holy woman. She fasts; she keeps the appropriate festivals. She is kind to everyone and God-fearing. Even the mention of her beauty is a sign that she is also holy. It is rare in the Bible that anyone is called beautiful who is not also virtuous.

Judith 8:9-27

⁹When Judith, therefore, heard of the harsh words which the people, discouraged by their lack of water, had spoken

against their ruler, and of all that Uzziah had said to them in
reply, swearing that he would hand over the city to the
Assyrians at the end of five days, ¹⁰she sent the maid who
was in charge of all her things to ask Uzziah, Chabris, and
Charmis, the elders of the city, to visit her. ¹¹When they
came, she said to them: "Listen to me, you rulers of the
people of Bethulia. What you said to the people today is not
proper. When you promised to hand over the city to our enemies at the end of five days unless within that time the
LORD comes to our aid, you interposed between God and
yourselves this oath which you took. ¹²Who are you, then,
that you should have put God to the test this day, setting
yourselves in the place of God in human affairs? ¹³It is the
LORD Almighty for whom you are laying down conditions;
will you never understand anything? ¹⁴You cannot plumb
the depths of the human heart or grasp the workings of the
human mind; how then can you fathom God, who has made
all these things, discern his mind, and understand his plan?

"No, my brothers, do not anger the LORD our God. ¹⁵For if
he does not wish to come to our aid within the five days, he
has it equally within his power to protect us at such time as
he pleases, or to destroy us in the face of our enemies. ¹⁶It is
not for you to make the LORD our God give surety for his
plans.

"God is not man that he should be moved by threats,
    nor human, that he may be given an ultimatum.

¹⁷"So while we wait for the salvation that comes from him,
let us call upon him to help us, and he will hear our cry if it
is his good pleasure. ¹⁸For there has not risen among us in
recent generations, nor does there exist today, any tribe, or
clan, or town, or city of ours that worships gods made by
hands, as happened in former days. ¹⁹It was for such conduct that our forefathers were handed over to the sword and
to pillage, and fell with great destruction before our enemies. ²⁰But since we acknowledge no other god but the
LORD, we hope that he will not disdain us or any of our
people. ²¹If we are taken, all Judea will fall, our sanctuary
will be plundered, and God will make us pay for its profa-
nation with our life's blood. ²²For the slaughter of our kinsmen, for the taking of exiles from the land, and for the
devastation of our inheritance, he will lay the guilt on our
heads. Wherever we shall be enslaved among the nations,

we shall be a mockery and a reproach in the eyes of our masters. [23]Our enslavement will not be turned to our benefit, but the LORD our God, will maintain it to our disgrace.

[24]"Therefore, my brothers, let us set an example for our kinsmen. Their lives depend on us, and the defense of the sanctuary, the temple, and the altar rests with us. [25]Besides all this, we should be grateful to the LORD our God, for putting us to the test, as he did our forefathers. [26]Recall how he dealt with Abraham, and how he tried Isaac, and all that happened to Jacob in Syrian Mesopotamia while he was tending the flocks of Laban, his mother's brother. [27]Not for vengeance did the LORD put them in the crucible to try their hearts, nor has he done so with us. It is by way of admonition that he chastises those who are close to him."

Judith has heard of the distress of her people. Holofernes has besieged the city and cut off the water supply. The people are beginning to collapse from thirst. She has also heard what the elders of the city have done. They, under the leadership of Uzziah, have given God five days within which to deliver them by sending help. If no help comes, they will hand over the city to the Assyrians. Judith sees the action of the elders as an act of despair. So she sends for the elders, chastises them for their failure to trust in God, reminds them of God's actions in the past, and exhorts them to courage. Her speech reveals that she is not only prayerful but also wise. She understands the ways of God. She is also fearless. She does not hesitate to summon and reprove even the elders of her city. She acts as a prophet, calling her people to radical faith in God, no matter how desperate the situation seems.

Judith 8:28-36

[28]Then Uzziah said to her: "All that you have said was spoken with good sense, and no one can gainsay your words. [29]Not today only is your wisdom made evident, but from your earliest years all the people have recognized your prudence, which corresponds to the worthy dispositions of your heart. [30]The people, however, were so tortured with thirst that they forced us to speak to them as we did, and to bind ourselves by an oath that we cannot break. [31]But now, God-fearing woman that you are, pray for us that the LORD

may send rain to fill up our cisterns, lest we be weakened still further."

32Then Judith said to them: "Listen to me! I will do something that will go down from generation to generation among the descendants of our race. 33Stand at the gate tonight to let me pass through with my maid; and within the days you have specified before you will surrender the city to our enemies, the LORD will rescue Israel by my hand. 34You must not inquire into what I am doing, for I will not tell you until my plan has been accomplished." 35Uzziah and the rulers said to her, "Go in peace, and may the LORD God go before you to take vengeance upon our enemies!" 36Then they withdrew from the tent and returned to their posts.

Uzziah still cannot comprehend the truth that God's ways are not our ways. He commends Judith for her words and then asks her to pray that God will answer in the way they desire by sending rain. Judith, on the other hand, has understood that the ways of God are often surprising. She also recognizes that our cooperation with God sometimes requires us to take unconventional risks. She will not tell Uzziah her plan; she gives him only the information necessary for his part in it. He must allow her to leave the city with her maid. She assures him that the oath he swore to the people will be honored, that God will deliver them within the time that he has set.

HER PRAYER

Judith 9:1-14

1Judith threw herself down prostrate, with ashes strewn upon her head, and wearing nothing over her sackcloth. While the incense was being offered in the temple of God in Jerusalem that evening, Judith prayed to the LORD with a loud voice: 2"LORD, God of my forefather Simeon! You put a sword into his hand to take revenge upon the foreigners who had immodestly loosened the maiden's girdle, shamefully exposed her thighs, and disgracefully violated her body. This they did, though you forbade it. 3Therefore you had their rulers slaughtered; and you covered with their blood the bed in which they lay deceived, the same bed that had felt the shame of their own deceiving. You smote the slaves together with their princes, and the princes together with their servants. ⁴Their wives you handed over to plunder, and their daughters to captivity; and all the spoils you divided among your favored sons, who burned with zeal for you, and in their abhorrence of the defilement of their kinswoman, called on you for help.

⁵"O God, my God, hear me also, a widow. It is you who were the author of those events and of what preceded and followed them. The present, also, and the future you have planned. Whatever you devise comes into being; ⁶the things you decide on come forward and say, 'Here we are!' All your ways are in readiness, and your judgment is made with foreknowledge.

⁷"Here are the Assyrians, a vast force, priding themselves on horse and rider, boasting of the power of their infantry, trusting in shield and spear, bow and sling. They do not know that

⁸"'You, the LORD, crush warfare;
   LORD is your name.'

"Shatter their strength in your might, and crush their force in your wrath; for they have resolved to profane your sanctuary, to defile the tent where your glorious name resides, and to overthrow with iron the horns of your altar. ⁹See their pride, and send forth your wrath upon their heads. Give me, a widow, the strong hand to execute my plan. ¹⁰With the guile of my lips, smite the slave together with the ruler, the ruler together with his servant; crush their pride by the hand of a woman.

¹¹"Your strength is not in numbers, nor does your power depend upon stalwart men; but you are the God of the lowly, the helper of the oppressed, the supporter of the weak, the protector of the forsaken, the savior of those without hope.

¹²"Please, please, God of my forefather, God of the heritage of Israel, LORD of heaven and earth, Creator of the waters, King of all you have created, hear my prayer! ¹³Let my guileful speech bring wound and wale on those who have planned dire things against your covenant, your holy temple, Mount Zion, and the homes your children have inherited. ¹⁴Let your whole nation and all the tribes know clearly that you are the God of all power and might, and that there is no other who protects the people of Israel but you alone."

Judith is a woman of prayer. She knows the proper rituals for laments and prayers of petition. She dresses herself in penitential garments, sackcloth and ashes. She prostrates herself, approaching the great God from a position of lowliness and submission. She prays at an established time of prayer, the hour when the incense is being offered in the Jerusalem temple. She has prepared for her prayer with care and attention.

The content of her prayer is also carefully formed. She begins in the traditional style of the lament with a cry to God (9:2). She recalls events in the past when the covenant people were victorious through God's help (9:2-4). Judith, a descendant of Simeon, recounts the story of the rapè of Jacob's daughter Dinah by Shechem which was avenged by her brothers Simeon and Levi (Genesis 34).[1] It is common in laments to tell a story of God's deliverance in the past in order to motivate God to help the people in the present crisis.

Then Judith comes to the heart of her plea: "O God, my God, hear me also, a widow." Her petition (9:5-7) is based on the contrast between her own weakness and God's power. It is God who is in charge of all time. It is God who is the great warrior, not these boastful Assyrians (9:7-9). This great God uses power, not for glory but for love of the lowly. The strength of this great God is exercised, not through the mighty but through the weak (9:11-12). Therefore she counts on God to use her, a widow, to defeat the mighty Assyrians (9:9-10).

Her conclusion (9:12-14) pulls all the threads together. She motivates God to act with five glorious titles which express God's relationship to her, to Israel, and to all creation. In addition, she points out that the enemy is really attacking God— God's covenant, God's temple, God's people. She acknowledges that the people have no help except in God. Finally, she appeals to God's honor. Through this victory all peoples will know that Israel's God is the God of all power and might. For all these reasons God should answer her petition to use her guileful speech and strong hand to defeat the enemy. Since she is a woman and a widow, it will be obvious to all that the victory really belongs to God.

---

[1]See chapter two for the story of Dinah.

Judith's prayer reveals the depth of her holiness and wisdom. She has a clear understanding that God is God and she is not. She also understands God's care for her and for her people. She knows her own worth. She is willing and able to be an instrument of God.

HER BEAUTY

Judith 10:1-10

1As soon as Judith had thus concluded, and ceased her invocation to the God of Israel, 2she rose from the ground. She called her maid and they went down into the house, which she used only on sabbaths and feast days. 3She took off the sackcloth she had on, laid aside the garments of her widowhood, washed her body with water, and anointed it with rich ointment. She arranged her hair and bound it with a fillet, and put on the festive attire she had worn while her husband, Manasseh, was living. 4She chose sandals for her feet, and put on her anklets, bracelets, rings, earrings, and all her other jewelry. Thus she made herself very beautiful, to captivate the eyes of all the men who should see her.

5She gave her maid a leather flask of wine and a cruse of oil. She filled a bag with roasted grain, fig cakes, bread and cheese; all these provisions she wrapped up and gave to the maid to carry.

6Then they went out to the gate of the city of Bethulia and found Uzziah and the elders of the city, Chabris and Charmis, standing there. 7When these men saw Judith transformed in looks and differently dressed, they were very much astounded at her beauty and said to her, 8"May the God of our fathers bring you to favor, and make your undertaking a success, for the glory of the Israelites and the exaltation of Jerusalem."

Judith bowed down to God. Then she said to them, 9"Order the gate of the city opened for me, that I may go to carry out the business we discussed." So they ordered the youths to open the gate for her as she requested. 10When they did so, Judith and her maid went out. The men of the city kept her in view as she went down the mountain and crossed the valley; then they lost sight of her.

With her most important preparation completed, Judith now turns to other necessities to carry out her plan. She will use the weapon of beauty and charm to deliver God's people from the enemy. She dresses carefully, "to captivate the eyes of all the men who should see her." Her preparations are successful. The men of her town are astounded at her beauty. She also enlists the help of her maid and prepares food so that they will not break the Jewish dietary laws by eating the food of the enemy. Thus armed, she sets out for the enemy camp.

She is an example to her fearful people of courage and trust in God. She and her maid go out to the enemy camp, depending completely on the power of God. Just as Israel had no defense but God at the Reed Sea, so Judith has nothing but God to protect her in the Assyrian camp. She has taken to heart the words of Ps 20:8-9: "Some rely on chariots, others on horses [the army vehicles of the ancient world], / but we on the name of the LORD our God. / They collapse and fall, / but we stand strong and firm."

HER WIT

Judith 10:11-19

11As Judith and her maid walked directly across the valley, they encountered the Assyrian outpost. 12The men took her in custody and asked her, "To what people do you belong? Where do you come from, and where are you going?" She replied: "I am a daughter of the Hebrews, and I am fleeing from them, because they are about to be delivered up to you as prey. 13I have come to see Holofernes, the general in chief of your forces, to give him a trustworthy report; I will show him the route by which he can ascend and take possession of the whole mountain district without a single one of his men suffering injury or loss of life."

14When the men heard her words and gazed upon her face, which appeared wondrously beautiful to them, they said to her, 15"By coming down thus promptly to see our master, you have saved your life. Now go to his tent; some of our men will accompany you to present you to him. 16When you stand before him, have no fear in your heart; give him the report you speak of, and he will treat you well." 17So they detailed a hundred of their men as an escort for her and her maid, and these conducted them to the tent of Holofernes.

18When the news of her arrival spread among the tents, a crowd gathered in the camp. They came and stood around her as she waited outside the tent of Holofernes, while he was being informed about her. 19They marveled at her beauty, regarding the Israelites with wonder because of her, and they said to one another, "Who can despise this people that has such women among them? It is not wise to leave one man of them alive, for if any were to be spared they could beguile the whole world."

It is not only the Israelite men who are astounded at Judith's beauty. The men of the Assyrian camp are equally dazed. For the sake of her beauty they admire her whole people: "Who can despise this people that has such women among them?" Her beauty has won her acceptance in the enemy camp.

Judith has also asked for a second weapon, guileful speech. She begins weaving her web of deceit by hinting that Holofernes will be successful. She can indeed show him a route by which he could conquer. He will not be able to do so, however, because the successful outcome of her plan will leave him dead.

Judith 10:20–11:23

20The guard of Holofernes and all his servants came out and ushered her into the tent. 21Now Holofernes was reclining on his bed under a canopy with a netting of crimson and gold, emeralds and other precious stones. 22When they announced her to him, he came out to the antechamber, preceded by silver lamps; 23and when Holofernes and his servants beheld Judith, they all marveled at the beauty of her face. She threw herself down prostrate before him, but his servants raised her up.

11:1Then Holofernes said to her: "Take courage, lady; have no fear in your heart! Never have I harmed anyone who chose to serve Nebuchadnezzar, king of all the earth. 2Nor would I have raised my spear against your people who dwell in the mountain region, had they not despised me and brought this upon themselves. 3But now tell me why you fled from them and came to us. In any case, you have come to safety. Take courage! Your life is spared tonight and for the future. 4No one at all will harm you. Rather, you will be

well treated, as are all the servants of my lord, King Nebuchadnezzar."

⁵Judith answered him: "Listen to the words of your servant,
and let your handmaid speak in your presence! I will tell no
lie to my lord this night, ⁶and if you follow out the words of
your handmaid, God will give you complete success, and
my lord will not fail in any of his undertakings. ⁷By the life
of Nebuchadnezzar, king of all the earth, and by the power
of him who has sent you to set all creatures aright! not only
do men serve him through you; but even the wild beasts
and the cattle and the birds of the air, because of your
strength, will live for Nebuchadnezzar and his whole house.
⁸Indeed, we have heard of your wisdom and sagacity, and
all the world is aware that throughout the kingdom you
alone are competent, rich in experience, and distinguished
in military strategy.

⁹"As for Achior's speech in your council, we have heard of
it. When the men of Bethulia spared him, he told them all he
had said to you. ¹⁰So then, my lord and master, do not disregard his word, but bear it in mind, for it is true. For our
people are not punished, nor does the sword prevail against
them, except when they sin against their God. ¹¹But now
their guilt has caught up with them by which they bring the
wrath of their God upon them whenever they do wrong; so
that my lord will not be repulsed and fail, but death will
overtake them. ¹²Since their food gave out and all their
water ran low, they decided to kill their animals, and determined to consume all the things which God in his laws forbade them to eat. ¹³They decreed that they would use up the
first fruits of grain and the tithes of wine and oil which they
had sanctified and reserved for the priests who minister in
the presence of our God in Jerusalem: things which no lay-
man should even touch with his hands. ¹⁴They have sent
messengers to Jerusalem to bring back to them authoriza-
tion from the council of the elders; for the inhabitants there
have also done these things. ¹⁵On the very day when the
response reaches them and they act upon it, they will be
handed over to you for destruction.

¹⁶"As soon as I, your handmaid, learned all this, I fled from
them. God has sent me to perform with you such deeds that
people throughout the world will be astonished on hearing
of them. ¹⁷Your handmaid is, indeed, a God-fearing woman,

serving the God of heaven night and day. Now I will remain with you, my lord; but each night your handmaid will go out to the ravine and pray to God. He will tell me when the Israelites have committed their crimes. [18]Then I will come and let you know, so that you may go out with your whole force, and not one of them will be able to withstand you. [19]I will lead you through Judea, till you come to Jerusalem, and there I will set up your judgment seat. You will drive them like sheep that have no shepherd, and not even a dog will growl at you. This was told me, and announced to me in advance, and I in turn have been sent to tell you."

[20]Her words pleased Holofernes and all his servants; they marveled at her wisdom and exclaimed, [21]"No other woman from one end of the world to the other looks so beautiful and speaks so wisely!" [22]Then Holofernes said to her: "God has done well in sending you ahead of your people, to bring victory to our arms, and destruction to those who have despised my lord. [23]You are fair to behold, and your words are well spoken. If you do as you have said, your God will be my God; you shall dwell in the palace of King Nebuchadnezzar, and shall be renowned throughout the earth."

The first two weapons in Judith's arsenal, beauty and wit, are wonderfully effective. Like the rest of the Assyrian camp, Holofernes marvels at her beauty. Her words, a mixture of truth and deceit, are even more powerful. The general is so vain that he interprets everything she says to his own benefit. When she says that she will tell no lie to her lord and that her lord will not fail in any of his undertakings, Holofernes assumes that she is speaking of him. But it is her Lord God who will not fail. She tells Holofernes that, if he follows her words, God will give him complete success. It is true, that if he follows her words and lives according to God's law, he will be successful. But she knows that he will not do this. She reports that Achior's testimony is reliable, Israel will only be defeated if they are sinful.[2] She warns Holofernes to trust this word. But then she suggests to him that perhaps the people are indeed

---

[2]The Book of Judith is based on the theology of the Book of Judges: When the people are faithful, they are also victorious; when they sin, they

sinful and thus Holofernes will be able to conquer them. He
hears what he wants to hear. He misses the possibility that
they may be faithful to God.

Finally she says to him, "God has sent me to perform with
you such deeds that people throughout the world will be
astonished on hearing of them." She warns him further that
she is God-fearing and prayerful. She tells him clearly where
the source of her power lies. She is faithful and therefore God
will grant her victory. Still he does not understand. Unaware
that he speaks his own disaster, he concludes their meeting:
"God has done well in sending you ahead of your people."
Indeed!

Judith 12:1-9

1Then he ordered them to lead her into the room where his
silverware was kept, and bade them set a table for her with
his own delicacies to eat and his own wine to drink. 2But
Judith said, "I will not partake of them, lest it be an occasion
of sin; but I shall be amply supplied from the things I
brought with me." 3Holofernes asked her: "But if your
provisions give out, where shall we get more of the same to
provide for you? None of your people are with us." 4Judith
answered him, "As surely as you, my lord, live, your handmaid will not use up her supplies till the LORD accomplishes
by my hand what he has determined."

5Then the servants of Holofernes led her into the tent, where
she slept till midnight. In the night watch just before dawn,
she rose 6and sent this message to Holofernes, "Give orders,
my lord, to let your handmaid go out for prayer." 7So
Holofernes ordered his bodyguard not to hinder her. Thus

---

are defeated. Judith has already declared to the elders that she expects
victory because the people have not turned away from the Lord to other
gods (Jdt 8:17-20). The reader can thus assume that the people have been
faithful, even though Judith suggests to Holofernes that they have broken
the dietary laws because they have no other food (Jdt 11:12-13). There are
indications that they in truth still have food that they are permitted to eat,
since Judith was able to provide herself with enough proper food for her
sojourn in the enemy camp. Judith's suggestion to Holofernes that they
are unfaithful can be assumed to be part of her deceit.

she stayed in the camp three days. Each night she went out to the ravine of Bethulia, where she washed herself at the spring of the camp. 8After bathing, she besought the LORD, the God of Israel, to direct her way for the triumph of his people. 9Then she returned purified to the tent, and remained there until her food was brought to her toward evening.

Judith continues to be faithful to her religious practices and to deceive Holofernes even when she tells the truth. She observes the Jewish dietary regulations scrupulously; she speaks truly when she tells the general that she will not run out of food before God works through her to accomplish the divine will. She also leaves the camp each evening to bathe and to pray. This practice not only demonstrates her fidelity, it will also provide her escape. Her daily schedule creates a way she can leave the camp without arousing the suspicion of the guards. Her wit continues to be a formidable weapon.

HER STRONG HAND

Judith 12:10–13:3

10On the fourth day Holofernes gave a banquet for his servants alone, to which he did not invite any of the officers. 11And he said to Bagoas, the eunuch in charge of his household: "Go and persuade this Hebrew woman in your care to come and to eat and drink with us. 12It would be a disgrace for us to have such a woman with us without enjoying her company. If we do not entice her, she will laugh us to scorn."

13So Bagoas left the presence of Holofernes, and came to Judith and said, "So fair a maiden should not be reluctant to come to my lord to be honored by him, to enjoy drinking wine with us, and to be like one of the Assyrian women who live in the palace of Nebuchadnezzar." 14She replied, "Who am I to refuse my lord? Whatever is pleasing to him I will promptly do. This will be a joy for me till the day of my death."

15Thereupon she proceeded to put on her festive garments and all her feminine adornments. Meanwhile her maid went ahead and spread out on the ground for her in front of Holofernes the fleece Bagoas had furnished for her daily use in reclining at her dinner. [16]Then Judith came in and reclined on it. The heart of Holofernes was in rapture over her, and his spirit was shaken. He was burning with the desire to possess her, for he had been biding his time to seduce her from the day he saw her. [17]Holofernes said to her, "Drink and be merry with us!" [18]Judith replied, "I will gladly drink, my lord, for at no time since I was born have I ever enjoyed life as much as I do today." [19]She then took the things her maid had prepared, and ate and drank in his presence. [20]Holofernes, charmed by her, drank a great quantity of wine, more than he had ever drunk on one single day in his life.

[13:1]When it grew late, his servants quickly withdrew. Bagoas closed the tent from the outside and excluded the attendants from their master's presence. They went off to their beds, for they were all tired from the prolonged banquet. [2]Judith was left alone in the tent with Holofernes, who lay prostrate on his bed, for he was sodden with wine. [3]She had ordered her maid to stand outside the bedroom and wait, as on the other days, for her to come out; she said she would be going out for her prayer. To Bagoas she had said this also.

The Assyrians have fatally misunderstood Judith. They have seen only her beauty and missed her wisdom. Holofernes sends his servant to bring Judith to his table and his bed, declaring that it would be a disgrace not to enjoy and take possession of such beauty. He has been waiting for a moment to seduce her. He is so intoxicated by her beauty that he becomes totally drunk on wine. It is the familiar story of lust and sexual conquest in which the woman becomes simply an object to satisfy the man's desire (e.g., Amnon and Tamar). In this story, however, it is the man himself who will be destroyed by his action. Holofernes' focus on Judith's beauty and disregard of her wit will be his undoing.

Judith, on the other hand, continues to use the weapons both of beauty and of wisdom. She adorns herself for the encounter. She makes true statements which would warn Holofernes if he were not blinded by arrogance. She declares that pleasing her Lord is a lasting joy to her; Holofernes assumes that he is her lord. She exclaims that this is the happiest day of her life; Holofernes does not realize that it is his anticipated death that gives her such delight. He has been lured into totally underestimating his enemy.

Judith 13:4-10

> 4When all had departed, and no one, small or great, was left in the bedroom, Judith stood by Holofernes' bed and said within herself: "O LORD, God of all might, in this hour look graciously on my undertaking for the exaltation of Jerusalem; 5now is the time for aiding your heritage and for carrying out my design to shatter the enemies who have risen against us." 6She went to the bedpost near the head of Holofernes, and taking his sword from it, 7drew close to the bed, grasped the hair of his head, and said, "Strengthen me this day, O God of Israel!" 8Then with all her might she struck him twice in the neck and cut off his head. 9She rolled his body off the bed and took the canopy from its supports. Soon afterward, she came out and handed over the head of Holofernes to her maid, 10who put it into her food pouch; and the two went off together as they were accustomed to do for prayer.

Finally the critical moment arrives. Holofernes is drunk on his bed. Everyone else has left. The time has come for the use of Judith's third weapon, her strong hand. She prepares herself with prayer, acknowledging again her conviction that it is through God's power that she acts. Strengthened by God, she beheads Holofernes. She uses his own sword, the weapon that has killed and subjugated so many people. She has accomplished what she set out to do. She has killed the enemy of her people. Through her, God has saved Israel.

When Judith emerges from Holofernes' tent, she hands the head to her maid who puts it into the food pouch. The maid is a valued partner in Judith's courageous enterprise. It was the maid who first summoned the elders to Judith's house. The maid helps with her initial preparations. The maid is her companion in the enemy camp and goes out with her to pray each evening. The maid prepares her for the final encounter with Holofernes and then stands guard. Now this brave woman accepts the severed head of the enemy from her mistress and calmly stows it away for the return journey to the camp. The maid, though often invisible and ignored, is essential to Judith's success.

Blessed Among Women

Judith 13:10-20

They passed through the camp, and skirting the ravine, reached Bethulia on the mountain. As they approached its gates, [11]Judith shouted to the guards from a distance: "Open! Open the gate! God, our God, is with us. Once more he has made manifest his strength in Israel and his power against our enemies; he has done it this very day." [12]When the citizens heard her voice, they quickly descended to their city gate and summoned the city elders. [13]All the people, from the least to the greatest, hurriedly assembled, for her return seemed unbelievable. They opened the gate and welcomed the two women. They made a fire for light; and when they gathered around the two, [14]Judith urged them with a loud voice: "Praise God, praise him! Praise God, who has not withdrawn his mercy from the house of Israel, but has shattered our enemies by my hand this very night." [15]Then she took the head out of the pouch, showed it to them, and said: "Here is the head of Holofernes, general in charge of the Assyrian army, and here is the canopy under which he lay in his drunkenness. The LORD struck him down by the hand of a woman. [16]As the LORD lives, who has protected me in the path I have followed, I swear that it was my face that seduced Holofernes to his ruin, and that he did not sin with me to my defilement or disgrace."

[17]All the people were greatly astonished. They bowed down and worshiped God, saying with one accord, "Blessed are you, our God, who today have brought to nought the enemies of your people." [18]Then Uzziah said to her: "Blessed are you, daughter, by the Most High God, above all the women on earth; and blessed be the LORD God, the creator of heaven and earth, who guided your blow at the head of the chief of our enemies. [19]Your deed of hope will never be forgotten by those who tell of the might of God. [20]May God make this redound to your everlasting honor, rewarding you with blessings, because you risked your life when your people were being oppressed, and you averted our disaster, walking uprightly before our God." And all the people answered, "Amen! Amen!"

When the two women arrive at the gate of Bethulia, the townspeople can hardly believe that they have been delivered from the enemy. Even as she demonstrates the truth of Holofernes' death, she urges the people to remember their true Deliverer: "Praise God!" The people respond to her exhortation and pray in thanksgiving and praise. She reminds them that God brings victory to the righteous; she assures them that she has not sinned with Holofernes (13:16). Uzziah, who thought deliverance could only come in the form of rain, adds praise of Judith to his praise of God. He honors her for risking her life and for acting as God's instrument of redemption. He calls her "blessed among women," recalling Jael who also killed an enemy general. The people's agreement sounds in their Amen.

The violence in Judith's action and the people's delight in her success may horrify and offend modern readers of the story. It is well to remember the deeper significance the author is trying to convey: No matter how helpless God's people are in the face of their enemies, God will deliver them. Christians see God's greatest deliverance in the death and resurrection of Jesus, an event in which horrible violence is overcome by absolute faith and undying love.

THE VICTORY

Judith 14:1-10

¹Then Judith said to them: "Listen to me, my brothers. Take this head and hang it on the parapet of your wall. ²At daybreak, when the sun rises on the earth, let each of you seize his weapons, and let all the able-bodied men rush out of the city under command of a captain, as if about to go down into the plain against the advance guard of the Assyrians, but without going down. ³They will seize their armor and hurry to their camp to awaken the generals of the Assyrian army. When they run to the tent of Holofernes and do not find him, panic will seize them, and they will flee before you. ⁴Then you and all the other inhabitants of the whole territory of Israel will pursue them and strike them down in their tracks. ⁵But before doing this, summon for me Achior the Ammonite, that he may see and recognize the one who despised the house of Israel and sent him here to meet his death."

⁶So they called Achior from the house of Uzziah. When he came and saw the head of Holofernes in the hand of one of

the men in the assembly of the people, he fell forward in a faint. ⁷Then, after they lifted him up, he threw himself at the feet of Judith in homage, saying: "Blessed are you in every tent of Judah; and in every foreign nation, all who hear of you will be struck with terror. ⁸But now, tell me all that you did during these days." So Judith told him, in the presence of the people, all that she had been doing from the day she left till the time she began speaking to them. ⁹When she finished her account, the people cheered loudly, and their city resounded with shouts of joy. ¹⁰Now Achior, seeing all that the God of Israel had done, believed firmly in him. He had the flesh of his foreskin circumcised, and he has been united with the house of Israel to the present day.

The victory is not yet complete, however; the Assyrian army is still encamped outside the city. Judith takes on the role of general and describes the plan of attack. She also sends for Achior, the leader of Israel's neighbor and sometime opponent, the Ammonites. Achior had been summoned by Holofernes when the Assyrians arrived at Bethulia to give information about the Israelites. Achior had reported that the Israelites are victorious when they are faithful to God but can be defeated when they are sinful (Jdt 5:5-24). Judith now needs him to witness to her fellow townspeople that the man she has beheaded is truly Holofernes. When Achior recognizes the head, he faints; then he joins in the praise of Judith. Her story leads him to faith in Israel's God. Achior is a dramatic contrast to Judith. The military man faints; the woman empowered by God overcomes the enemy.

Judith 14:11–15:3

¹¹At daybreak they hung the head of Holofernes on the wall. Then all the Israelite men took up their arms and went to the slopes of the mountain. ¹²When the Assyrians saw them, they notified their captains; these, in turn, went to the generals and division leaders and all their other commanders. ¹³They came to the tent of Holofernes and said to the one in charge of all his things, "Waken our master, for the slaves have dared come down to give us battle, to their utter destruction." ¹⁴Bagoas went in, and knocked at the entry of the tent, presuming that he was sleeping with Judith. ¹⁵As no

one answered, he parted the curtains, entered the bedroom, and found him lying on the floor, a headless corpse. [16]He broke into a loud clamor of weeping, groaning, and howling, and rent his garments. [17]Then he entered the tent where Judith had her quarters; and, not finding her, he rushed out to the troops and cried: [18]"The slaves have duped us! A single Hebrew woman has brought disgrace on the house of King Nebuchadnezzar. Here is Holofernes headless on the ground!"

[19]When the commanders of the Assyrian army heard these words, they rent their tunics and were seized with consternation. Loud screaming and howling arose in the camp.

[15:1]On hearing what had happened, those still in their tents were amazed, [2]and overcome with fear and trembling. No one kept ranks any longer; they scattered in all directions, and fled along every road, both through the valley and in the mountains. [3]Those also who were stationed in the mountain district around Bethulia took to flight. Then all the Israelite warriors overwhelmed them.

The Assyrians realize too late that Judith is more than beauty. Holofernes' servant, still blindly assuming that his master is sleeping with Judith, discovers instead the headless corpse. A search reveals that Judith has escaped. Only then does he recognize the truth of Judith's power: "A single Hebrew woman has brought disgrace on the house of King Nebuchadnezzar." His announcement is the final blow for the Assyrian army and they flee in disorder. A single Hebrew woman has won the victory for God.

Judith 15:4-13

[4]Uzziah sent messengers to Betomasthaim, to Choba and Kona, and to the whole country of Israel to report what had happened, that all might fall upon the enemy and destroy them. [5]On hearing this, all the Israelites, with one accord, attacked them and cut them down as far as Choba. Even those from Jerusalem and the rest of the mountain region took part in this, for they too had been notified of the happenings in the camp of their enemies. The Gileadites and the Galileans struck the enemy's flanks with great slaughter, even beyond Damascus and its territory. [6]The remaining

inhabitants of Bethulia swept down on the camp of the Assyrians, plundered it, and acquired great riches. 7The Israelites who returned from the slaughter took possession of what was left, till the towns and villages in the mountains and on the plain were crammed with the enormous quantity of booty they had seized.

8The high priest Joakim and the elders of the Israelites, who dwelt in Jerusalem, came to see for themselves the good things that the LORD had done for Israel, and to meet and congratulate Judith. 9When they had visited her, all with one accord blessed her, saying:

> "You are the glory of Jerusalem,
>   the surpassing joy of Israel;
>   You are the splendid boast of our people.
> 10With your own hand you have done all this;
>   You have done good to Israel,
>   and God is pleased with what you have wrought.
> May you be blessed by the LORD Almighty
>   forever and ever!"

And all the people answered, "Amen!"

11For thirty days the whole populace plundered the camp, giving Judith the tent of Holofernes, with all his silver, his couches, his dishes, and all his furniture, which she accepted. She harnessed her mules, hitched her wagons to them, and loaded these things on them.

12All the women of Israel gathered to see her; and they blessed her and performed a dance in her honor. She took branches in her hands and distributed them to the women around her, 13and she and the other women crowned themselves with garlands of olive leaves. At the head of all the people, she led the women in the dance, while the men of Israel followed in their armor, wearing garlands and singing hymns.

The Israelite army completes the defeat of the Assyrians and returns to Bethulia loaded with goods. For a month all the people of Israel (cf. 15:4-6) celebrate the victory. They plunder the camp and give Judith what belonged to Holofernes. The women bless Judith and dance in her honor; the men, dressed in their armor, sing hymns. The Jerusalem priests and elders also bless her.

The priestly blessing of Judith is often used for feasts of Mary. Mary, too, is the glory of Jerusalem and the joy of Israel. Mary, too, is the instrument of God's victory. She has given birth to the redeemer who saves his people from their mortal enemy. God is pleased with what she has done. Mary, too, is blessed among women as Uzziah proclaims of Judith: "Blessed are you, daughter, by the Most High God, above all the women on earth; and blessed be the LORD God, the creator of heaven and earth, who guided your blow at the head of the chief of our enemies" (13:18). Mary, too, is blessed by the Lord Almighty forever and ever.

THE VICTORY SONG

Judith 15:14–16:17

14Judith led all Israel in this song of thanksgiving, and the people swelled this hymn of praise:

16:1"Strike up the instruments,
  a song to my God with timbrels,
  chant to the LORD with cymbals;
Sing to him a new song,
  exalt and acclaim his name.
2For the LORD is God; he crushes warfare,
  and sets his encampment among his people;
  he snatched me from the hands of my persecutors.

3"The Assyrian came from the mountains of the north,
  with the myriads of his forces he came;
Their numbers blocked the torrents,
  their horses covered the hills.
4He threatened to burn my land,
  put my youths to the sword,
Dash my babes to the ground,
  make my children a prey,
  and seize my virgins as spoil.

5"But the LORD Almighty thwarted them,
  by a woman's hand he confounded them.
6Not by youths was their mighty one struck down,
  nor did titans bring him low,
  nor huge giants attack him;
But Judith, the daughter of Merari,
  by the beauty of her countenance disabled him.

⁷She took off her widow's garb
  to raise up the afflicted in Israel.
She anointed her face with fragrant oil;
    ⁸with a fillet she fastened her tresses,
    and put on a linen robe to beguile him.
⁹Her sandals caught his eyes,
    and her beauty captivated his mind.
    The sword cut through his neck.

¹⁰"The Persians were dismayed at her daring,
    the Medes appalled at her boldness.
¹¹When my lowly ones shouted, they were terrified;
    when my weaklings cried out, they trembled;
    at the sound of their war cry, they took to flight.
¹²Sons of slave girls pierced them through;
    the supposed sons of rebel mothers cut them down;
    they perished before the ranks of my LORD.

¹³"A new hymn I will sing to my God.
    O LORD, great are you and glorious,
    wonderful in power and unsurpassable.
¹⁴Let your every creature serve you;
    for you spoke, and they were made,
You sent forth your spirit, and they were created;
    no one can resist your word.
¹⁵The mountains to their bases, and the seas, are shaken;
    the rocks, like wax, melt before your glance.

"But to those who fear you,
    you are very merciful.
¹⁶Though the sweet odor of every sacrifice is a trifle,
    and the fat of all holocausts but little in your sight,
    one who fears the LORD is forever great.

¹⁷"Woe to the nations that rise against my people!
    the LORD Almighty will requite them;
    in the day of judgment he will punish them:
He will send fire and worms into their flesh,
    and they shall burn and suffer forever."

Judith's story is framed by prayer (cf. Judith 9). Throughout her daring exploit and the congratulations that follow, she continues to declare that she did not act through her own power but through the power of God. She consistently turns her people's praise of her to praise of God.

After the victory is won, Judith takes up the role of women in the Holy War tradition. Miriam led the women in song and dance after their escape from Egypt (Exod 15:20-21). Deborah led the song of praise after the defeat of Sisera (Judg 5:1). Jephthah's daughter, whose story ends in tragedy, comes out to celebrate her father's victory over the Ammonites (Judg 11:34). Judith leads the song of thanksgiving in praise of God who has delivered the people from the Assyrians.

Judith's song begins as a hymn. There is a call to praise God (16:1-2) and the reasons for praise (16:2). The story of the victory is told as an extended reason for praise (16:3-12). The final section stretches the form as God is addressed directly (16:13-15, not common in hymns). The song ends with praise of God-fearers and a woe upon their enemies (16:16-17). Original material is found in the description of victory (16:3-12); the remaining verses echo material from the Books of Judges, Psalms, and Isaiah. In verses 3-12, Judith's beauty is highlighted as the weapon which disabled the enemy. The first and last sections (16:1-2, 13-17) set Judith's action in the context of God's continued protection of the people.

RESPECTED WIDOW

Judith 16:18-25

18The people then went to Jerusalem to worship God; when they were purified, they offered their holocausts, freewill offerings, and gifts. 19Judith dedicated, as a votive offering to God, all the things of Holofernes that the people had given her, as well as the canopy that she herself had taken from his bedroom. 20For three months the people continued their celebration in Jerusalem before the sanctuary, and Judith remained with them.

21When those days were over, each one returned to his inheritance. Judith went back to Bethulia and remained on her estate. For the rest of her life she was renowned throughout the land. 22Many wished to marry her, but she gave herself to no man all the days of her life from the time of the death and burial of her husband, Manasseh. 23She lived to be very old in the house of her husband, reaching the advanced age of a hundred and five. She died in Bethulia, where they buried her in the tomb of her husband, Manasseh; 24and the house of Israel mourned her for seven days. Before she died, she distributed her goods to the relatives of her husband, Manasseh, and to her own relatives; and to the maid she gave her freedom.

25During the life of Judith and for a long time after her death, no one again disturbed the Israelites.

At the conclusion of the story we find Judith again at home, an honored and respected widow. She arranges all her affairs with wisdom. She donates the spoil from Holofernes to the sanctuary. She distributes her wealth to her relatives and those of her husband. She gives the faithful maid her freedom. The final sentence ranks her with the judges, those men and women who saved Israel from their enemies during the pioneer period (cf. Judg 3:11, 30; 5:31; 8:28). Her long life is a sign of God's blessing upon her and upon the people. As long as she lives, and even afterwards, they have peace. She is the glory of Jerusalem, the joy of Israel, the splendid boast of her people.

SUSANNA

Attached to the Book of Daniel are two stories in Greek, the story of Susanna (Daniel 13) and the story of Bel and the Dragon (Daniel 14). These stories are intended to entertain and to edify their readers and to demonstrate, as the rest of the Book of Daniel does, that no matter what distress afflicts God's people, God will win in the end.

A FAITHFUL WIFE

Daniel 13:1-4

1In Babylon there lived a man named Joakim, 2who married a very beautiful and God-fearing woman, Susanna, the daughter of Hilkiah; 3her pious parents had trained their daughter according to the law of Moses. 4Joakim was very rich; he had a garden near his house, and the Jews had recourse to him often because he was the most respected of them all.

The story begins by introducing the central character, Susanna, and her husband Joakim. Susanna is beautiful, God-fearing, and well-trained in the law. She is a model Jewish woman. Her husband Joakim is rich and respected. The couple are living in exile, and thus become an example to Jews living outside of Israel of how a faithful life can be lived in any place.

Daniel 13:5-14

5That year, two elders of the people were appointed judges, of whom the Lord said, "Wickedness has come out of Babylon: from the elders who were to govern the people as judges." 6These men, to whom all brought their cases, frequented the house of Joakim. 7When the people left at noon, Susanna used to enter her husband's garden for a walk. 8When the old men saw her enter every day for her walk, they began to lust for her. 9They suppressed their consciences; they would not allow their eyes to look to heaven, and did not keep in mind just judgments. 10Though both were enamored of her, they did not tell each other their trouble, 11for they were ashamed to reveal their lustful desire to have her. 12Day by day they watched eagerly for her. 13One day they said to each other, "Let us be off for home, it is time for lunch." So they went out and parted; 14but both turned back, and when they met again, they asked each other the reason. They admitted their lust, and then they agreed to look for an occasion when they could meet her alone.

The peaceful scene does not last long. Two official representatives of the religious tradition, thus expected to be both wise and holy, are neither. These two judges lust after Susanna. Not only that, they nourish their lust and avoid prayer lest the lust be diminished. Their consciences cannot be completely suppressed, however, and so each is ashamed to tell the other of his desire. But one day they catch each other looking for Susanna and reveal their evil intentions. Now they conspire together to find Susanna alone. Through all their scheming there is no hint that Susanna has encouraged their lust, nor that she even suspects it.

A COURAGEOUS WIFE

Daniel 13:15-27

15One day, while they were waiting for the right moment, she entered the garden as usual, with two maids only. She decided to bathe, for the weather was warm. 16Nobody else was there except the two elders, who had hidden themselves and were watching her. 17"Bring me oil and soap," she said to the maids, "and shut the garden doors while I bathe." 18They did as she said; they shut the garden doors and left by the side gate to fetch what she had ordered, unaware that the elders were hidden inside.

19As soon as the maids had left, the two old men got up and hurried to her. 20"Look," they said, "the garden doors are shut, and no one can see us; give in to our desire, and lie with us. 21If you refuse, we will testify against you that you dismissed your maids because a young man was here with you."

22"I am completely trapped," Susanna groaned. "If I yield, it will be my death; if I refuse, I cannot escape your power. 23Yet it is better for me to fall into your power without guilt than to sin before the Lord." 24Then Susanna shrieked, and the old men also shouted at her, 25as one of them ran to open the garden doors. 26When the people in the house heard the cries from the garden, they rushed in by the side gate to see what had happened to her. 27At the accusations by the old men, the servants felt very much ashamed, for never had any such thing been said about Susanna.

The two old men find their opportunity. Susanna is alone in the garden bathing. They approach her, expecting certain conquest. If Susanna will not submit to their lust, they will testify to her adultery with another man. In Israelite law the testimony of two witnesses was sufficient to convict. If Susanna resists she will certainly be convicted of adultery and executed by stoning (Lev 20:10; Deut 22:22-24). If she submits she is guilty of the crime which is worthy of death. It seems she cannot win.

The two elders, however, have underestimated Susanna's strength, her virtue. She entrusts her case to God and sounds the alarm. The old men stand by their word and accuse her of adultery. Their accusation is apparently believed, even though the servants know that no such thing has ever been said about Susanna. It seems Susanna faces certain execution.

AN ACCUSED WIFE

Daniel 13:28-43

28When the people came to her husband Joakim the next day, the two wicked elders also came, fully determined to put Susanna to death. Before all the people they ordered: 29"Send for Susanna, the daughter of Hilkiah, the wife of Joakim." When she was sent for, 30she came with her parents, children and all her relatives. 31Susanna, very delicate and beautiful, 32was veiled; but those wicked men ordered her to uncover her face so as to sate themselves with her beauty. 33All her relatives and the onlookers were weeping.

34In the midst of the people the two elders rose up and laid their hands on her head. 35Through her tears she looked up to heaven, for she trusted in the Lord wholeheartedly. 36The elders made this accusation: "As we were walking in the garden alone, this woman entered with two girls and shut the doors of the garden, dismissing the girls. 37A young man, who was hidden there, came and lay with her. 38When we, in a corner of the garden, saw this crime, we ran toward them. 39We saw them lying together, but the man we could not hold, because he was stronger than we; he opened the doors and ran off. 40Then we seized this one and asked who the young man was, 41but she refused to tell us. We testify to this." The assembly believed them, since they were elders and judges of the people, and they condemned her to death.

42But Susanna cried aloud: "O eternal God, you know what is hidden and are aware of all things before they come to be: 43you know that they have testified falsely against me. Here I am about to die, though I have done none of the things with which these wicked men have charged me."

The trial is convened. The accused appears with all her relatives for support. The accusers demand that she be unveiled so that they can continue to inflame their lust even as they condemn her to death. Their fatal testimony is delivered. Both the men and Susanna are esteemed in the community.

When the people are faced with a choice of whom to believe, the status of the men weighs more heavily than Susanna's virtue. They condemn Susanna to death. Susanna turns, not to any human defender, but to God. God knows the charges are false. God is the only one who can deliver her.

HER REDEEMER

Daniel 13:44-59

44The Lord heard her prayer. 45As she was being led to execution, God stirred up the holy spirit of a young boy named Daniel, 46and he cried aloud: "I will have no part in the death of this woman." 47All the people turned and asked him, "What is this you are saying?" 48He stood in their midst and continued, "Are you such fools, O Israelites! To condemn a woman of Israel without examination and without clear evidence? 49Return to court, for they have testified falsely against her."

50Then all the people returned in haste. To Daniel the elders said, "Come, sit with us and inform us, since God has given you the prestige of old age." 51But he replied, "Separate these two far from one another that I may examine them."

52After they were separated one from the other, he called one of them and said: "How you have grown evil with age! Now have your past sins come to term: 53passing unjust sentences, condemning the innocent, and freeing the guilty, although the Lord says, 'The innocent and the just you shall not put to death.' 54Now, then, if you were a witness, tell me under what tree you saw them together." 55"Under a mastic tree," he answered. "Your fine lie has cost you your head," said Daniel; "for the angel of God shall receive the sentence from him and split you in two." 56Putting him to one side, he ordered the other one to be brought. "Offspring of Canaan, not of Judah," Daniel said to him, "beauty has seduced you, lust has subverted your conscience. 57This is how you acted with the daughters of Israel, and in their fear they yielded to you; but a daughter of Judah did not tolerate your wickedness. 58Now then, tell me under what tree you surprised them together." 59"Under an oak," he said. "Your fine lie has cost you also your head," said Daniel; "for the angel of God waits with a sword to cut you in two so as to make an end of you both."

God does not fail Susanna. But as usual God works through an unlikely human being to minister justice. God sends a young man to bring divine wisdom to the situation. Daniel demands that the case be reopened. He cross-examines the two elders separately and convicts them of false witness. Susanna is vindicated and delivered from death.

Daniel 13:60-64

60The whole assembly cried aloud, blessing God who saves those that hope in him. 61They rose up against the two elders, for by their own words Daniel had convicted them of perjury. According to the law of Moses, they inflicted on them the penalty they had plotted to impose on their neighbor: 62they put them to death. Thus was innocent blood spared that day.

63Hilkiah and his wife praised God for their daughter Susanna, as did Joakim her husband and all her relatives, because she was found innocent of any shameful deed. 64And from that day onward Daniel was greatly esteemed by the people.

The conclusion of the story restores the scene to its tranquility. The elders are condemned to the death they had plotted for Susanna. Susanna's reputation is restored. The young Daniel gains great respect. Everyone lives happily ever after!

Susanna is an example of a virtuous woman who trusts God with her life. She makes only two speeches in the entire story. The first declares her commitment to remain faithful to God and to her husband (13:22-23); the second is her cry to God for help (13:42-43). She leads the ordinary life of a wealthy respected woman until the crucial moment in the garden. The crisis reveals the depth of her beauty and of her fidelity. She ranks with Judith as a woman who, by faith, defeats the enemies of her people. These two women are used by God to save the people from enemies both within (fellow Jews) and without (foreigners). Of both women it can be said, "You are the glory of Jerusalem, the surpassing joy of Israel" (Jdt 15:9).

9. Queen Esther

Suggested Readings: Book of Esther.

The Book of Esther has a unique biblical history. The Hebrew version never mentions the name of God. Perhaps for this reason the book was not accepted into the canon of the Hebrew Bible until the third century C.E. It is the only book of the Hebrew Bible not found among the scrolls at Qumran. The Septuagint, the Greek version of the Old Testament, contains several additions to the story, which make explicit mention of God.[1] The additions are found in the Roman Catholic and Orthodox canon. Other Christian Bibles contain the Hebrew version.

The Book of Esther is a tale told to edify the hearers. It is a melodrama in which the hero and the villain are painted in bold colors. The story is set in fifth-century Persia and the first telling of the story may date to the same century. In the Hebrew version of the story, the faithful Jews of the Diaspora, living outside of Israel, carry the hidden presence of God and are the ministers of God's providence. The Greek additions contain prayers addressed to God and an apocalyptic dream sequence explaining the Jews' vengeance on their enemies. What was subtly suggested in the Hebrew story is clearly stated in the Greek additions.

A DEPOSED QUEEN

Esther 1:9-22

> 9Queen Vashti also gave a feast for the women inside the royal palace of King Ahasuerus.

[1]The Greek additions are numbered either as chapters A–F or as 10:4–16:24. This commentary follows the numbering of the New American Bible (chs. A–F).

[10]On the seventh day, when the king was merry with wine, he instructed Mehuman, Biztha, Harbona, Bigtha, Abagtha, Zethar, and Carkas, the seven eunuchs who attended King Ahasuerus, [11]to bring Queen Vashti into his presence wearing the royal crown, that he might display her beauty to the populace and the officials, for she was lovely to behold. [12]But Queen Vashti refused to come at the royal order issued through the eunuchs. At this the king's wrath flared up, and he burned with fury. [13]He conferred with the wise men versed in the law, because the king's business was conducted in general consultation with lawyers and jurists. [14]He summoned Carshena, Shethar, Admatha, Tarshish, Meres, Marsena and Memucan, the seven Persian and Median officials who were in the king's personal service and held first rank in the realm, [15]and asked them, "What is to be done by law with Queen Vashti for disobeying the order of King Ahasuerus issued through the eunuchs?"

[16]In the presence of the king and of the officials, Memucan answered: "Queen Vashti has not wronged the king alone, but all the officials and the populace throughout the provinces of King Ahasuerus. [17]For the queen's conduct will become known to all the women, and they will look with disdain upon their husbands when it is reported, 'King Ahasuerus commanded that Queen Vashti be ushered into his presence, but she would not come.' [18]This very day the Persian and Median ladies who hear of the queen's conduct will rebel against all the royal officials, with corresponding disdain and rancor. [19]If it please the king, let an irrevocable royal decree be issued by him and inscribed among the laws of the Persians and Medes, forbidding Vashti to come into the presence of King Ahasuerus and authorizing the king to give her royal dignity to one more worthy than she. [20]Thus, when the decree which the king will issue is published throughout his realm, vast as it is, all wives will honor their husbands, from the greatest to the least."

[21]This proposal found acceptance with the king and the officials, and the king acted on the advice of Memucan. [22]He sent letters to all the royal provinces, to each province in its own script and to each people in its own language, to the effect that every man should be lord in his own home.

The Persian court under Ahasuerus (Xerxes I, 485–464 B.C.E.)[2] is the scene of great wealth and high banqueting. The king holds a seven-day feast and at the same time Queen Vashti holds a feast for the women. On the seventh and final day of the banquets, the king orders Vashti to appear at the men's banquet. He has displayed the rest of his wealth; now he desires to display the beauty of his queen.

Vashti is supposed to come "wearing the royal crown." There is a rabbinic tradition that she was supposed to come, wearing nothing but the royal crown. In any case, her only function is to enhance the glory of the king whose possession she is.

Vashti refuses to come. Her refusal creates a storm of protest among the king's advisers far beyond the significance of the event. Their great fear is that her assertion of independence will encourage other wives to assert independence also. The absolute power of husbands over their wives will be in question.

The scene is a satire. Everything is exaggerated. The wealth is overwhelming. The banquets are celebrations of gluttony. The demand of the king is arbitrary. The response of the courtiers is overdrawn. The only sensible person in the scene seems to be Vashti. Nonetheless Vashti is deposed and the stage is set for the search for a new queen.

A BEAUTIFUL YOUNG VIRGIN

Esther 2:1-7

[1]After this, when King Ahasuerus' wrath had cooled, he thought over what Vashti had done and what had been decreed against her. [2]Then the king's personal attendants suggested: "Let beautiful young virgins be sought for the king. [3]Let the king appoint commissaries in all the provinces of his realm to bring together all beautiful young virgins to the harem in the stronghold of Susa. Under the care of the royal eunuch Hegai, custodian of the women, let cosmetics be given them. [4]Then the girl who pleases the king shall reign

---

[2]The story told in this book is found nowhere in the Persian records of the reign of Ahasuerus (Xerxes).

in place of Vashti." This suggestion pleased the king, and he acted accordingly.

5There was in the stronghold of Susa a certain Jew named Mordecai, son of Jair, son of Shimei, son of Kish, a Benjaminite, 6who had been exiled from Jerusalem with the captives taken with Jeconiah, king of Judah, whom Nebuchadnezzar, king of Babylon, had deported. 7He was foster father to Hadassah, that is, Esther, his cousin; for she had lost both father and mother. The girl was beautifully formed and lovely to behold. On the death of her father and mother, Mordecai had taken her as his own daughter.

Esther is introduced in the context of the search for a queen. She is a Jew, an orphan, and very beautiful. Her Hebrew name is Hadassah, the myrtle plant, symbol of thanksgiving and peace. Her Persian name, Esther, is a variant of Ishtar, the Babylonian goddess of fertility. She has been adopted by her cousin Mordecai who has become her protector.

Esther 2:8-11

8When the king's order and decree had been obeyed and many maidens brought together to the stronghold of Susa under the care of Hegai, Esther also was brought in to the royal palace under the care of Hegai, custodian of the women. 9The girl pleased him and won his favor. So he promptly furnished her with cosmetics and provisions. Then picking out seven maids for her from the royal palace, he transferred both her and her maids to the best place in the harem. 10Esther did not reveal her nationality or family, for Mordecai had commanded her not to do so.

11Day by day Mordecai would walk about in front of the court of the harem, to learn how Esther was faring and what was to become of her.

Esther is beautiful; she also has a pleasing personality. She immediately wins the favor of the eunuch who is put in charge of the harem. His assistance will prove invaluable to her. She seems docile as she participates in the beauty treatments preparing her to go to the king. As the story progresses, she will be challenged to act assertively. She conceals her Jewish identity which sets up the conflict of the story. Her revelation to the king that she is a Jew will be the turning point of the plot.

THE BEAUTY CONTEST

Esther 2:12-18

[12]Each girl went in turn to visit King Ahasuerus after the twelve months' preparation decreed for the women. Of this period of beautifying treatment, six months were spent with oil of myrrh, and the other six months with perfumes and cosmetics. [13]Then, when the girl was to visit the king, she was allowed to take with her from the harem to the royal palace whatever she chose. [14]She would go in the evening and return in the morning to a second harem under the care of the royal eunuch Shaashgaz, custodian of the concubines. She could not return to the king unless he was pleased with her and had her summoned by name.

[15]As for Esther, daughter of Abihail and adopted daughter of his nephew Mordecai, when her turn came to visit the king, she did not ask for anything but what the royal eunuch Hegai, custodian of the women, suggested. Yet she won the admiration of all who saw her. [16]Esther was led to King Ahasuerus in his palace in the tenth month, Tebeth, in the seventh year of his reign. [17]The king loved Esther more than all other women, and of all the virgins she won his favor and benevolence. So he placed the royal diadem on her head and made her queen in place of Vashti. [18]Then the king gave a great feast in honor of Esther to all his officials and ministers, granting a holiday to the provinces and bestowing gifts with royal bounty.

The preparation for this royal beauty contest lasts a whole year. Esther participates along with the other young women in the anointings and instructions in the use of perfumes and cosmetics. Attention seems to be given only to external beauty.

When Esther is taken in to sleep with the king, she relies completely on the advice of the eunuch Hegai. She trusts him to know what will please the king. Her beauty is admired by all who see her. The king's decision affirms their opinion. The king is won by Esther and names her queen in place of Vashti.

Esther has won the favor *(hesed)* of the eunuch Hegai (2:9) and the admiration *(hen)* of the people (2:15). She has won the favor and devotion *(hen* and *hesed)* of the king (2:17). The phrase is a clue to what will happen later in the story. She is like Joseph who found favor *(hen)* in the sight of Potiphar and brought blessing to his house (Gen 39:4). God also showed kindness *(hesed)* to Joseph by giving him favor *(hen)* in the sight of the chief jailer and brought success to all that he did (Gen 39:21). She is like Ruth, a woman of faithful love *(hesed,* Ruth 3:10), who finds favor *(hen)* in the sight of Boaz (Ruth 2:2, 10, 13) and brings blessing to his house. Esther will again win the favor *(hen)* of the king and thus will be able to save her people (5:2, 8; 7:3; 8:5).

At this point of the story, however, Esther's character has not yet been revealed. Has the king simply replaced a beautiful independent queen with a beautiful docile queen? Will Esther make any difference in the life of Persia or in the life of her fellow Jews? Is her beauty only skin deep, or is there inner beauty as well?

Impending Danger

Esther 2:19-23

> 19[To resume: From the time the virgins had been brought together, and while Mordecai was passing his time at the king's gate, 20Esther had not revealed her family or nationality, because Mordecai had told her not to; and Esther continued to follow Mordecai's instructions, just as she had when she was being brought up by him. 21And during the time that Mordecai spent at the king's gate, Bagathan and Thares, two of the royal eunuchs who guarded the entrance, had plotted in anger to lay hands on King Ahasuerus. 22When the plot became known to Mordecai, he told Queen Esther, who in turn informed the king for Mordecai. 23The matter was investigated and verified, and both of them were hanged on a gibbet. This was written in the annals for the king's use.]

The first clue to the difference that Esther will make comes in a note concerning Mordecai's discovery of a plot to assassinate the king. Mordecai reports the plot to Esther who in turn informs the king. The traitors are executed and the affair recorded in the royal annals. The king's re-discovery of Mordecai's act will bring the conflict between Mordecai the Jew and Haman, their enemy, to a head (Est 6:1-11). Esther's action is that of intermediary. She still has not become a character in her own right.

The conflict between Mordecai and Haman is described in chapter three. Haman, raised to high rank by the king, demands that all the king's servants at the royal gate kneel and bow down to him. Mordecai refuses to do so. The reason he gives is that he is a Jew. Presumably he is making the point that he bows to God alone. Haman, enraged by Mordecai's refusal to bow to him, seeks an opportunity to destroy all the Jews in Ahasuerus' kingdom. He persuades the king to issue a decree that on a single day all the Jews of the kingdom should be killed. The day, chosen by lot (cf. Est 9:24-26), is the thirteenth day of the twelfth month, the month of Adar.

Esther 4:1-9

1When Mordecai learned all that was happening, he tore his garments, put on sackcloth and ashes, and walked through the city crying out loudly and bitterly, 2till he came before the royal gate, which no one clothed in sackcloth might enter. 3(Likewise in each of the provinces, wherever the king's legal enactment reached, the Jews went into deep mourning, with fasting, weeping, and lament; they all slept on sackcloth and ashes.)

4Queen Esther's maids and eunuchs came and told her. Overwhelmed with anguish, she sent garments for Mordecai to put on, so that he might take off his sackcloth; but he refused. 5Esther then summoned Hathach, one of the king's eunuchs whom he had placed at her service, and commanded him to find out what this action of Mordecai meant and the reason for it. 6So Hathach went out to Mordecai in the public square in front of the royal gate, 7and Mordecai told him all that had happened, as well as the exact amount of silver Haman had promised to pay to the royal treasury for the slaughter of the Jews. 8He also gave him a copy of the written decree for their destruction which had been promulgated in Susa, to show and explain to Esther. He was to instruct her to go to the king; she was to plead and intercede with him in behalf of her people. B4:8"Remember the days of your lowly estate," Mordecai had him say, "when you were brought up in my charge; for Haman, who is second to the king, has asked for our death. B4:9Invoke the LORD and speak to the king for us: save us from death."

9Hathach returned to Esther and told her what Mordecai had said.

Esther's transformation begins in chapter four. First of all, she seems to be embarrassed by Mordecai's sackcloth and ashes. Without determining the reason for his penance, she attempts to end his public display. It is also evident that the news of the royal decree authorizing the slaughter of the Jews has reached the provinces but has not reached the queen. She is not privy to the king's decisions, nor is she provided with the ordinary news of the kingdom.

It is Mordecai, through her eunuch, who must inform Esther of the impending danger. He suggests that she, too, is in danger; he refers to "her people" and "our death." He also gives her instructions. She is to plead both with the king and with God. Esther is still dependent on Mordecai for both information and direction.

FOR A TIME LIKE THIS

Esther 4:10-17

10Then Esther replied to Hathach and gave him this message for Mordecai: 11"All the servants of the king and the people of his provinces know that any man or woman who goes to the king in the inner court without being summoned, suffers the automatic penalty of death, unless the king extends to him the golden scepter, thus sparing his life. Now as for me, I have not been summoned to the king for thirty days."

12When Esther's words were reported to Mordecai, 13he had this reply brought to her: "Do not imagine that because you are in the king's palace, you alone of all the Jews will escape. 14Even if you now remain silent, relief and deliverance will come to the Jews from another source; but you and your father's house will perish. Who knows but that it was for a time like this that you obtained the royal dignity?"

15Esther sent back to Mordecai the response: 16"Go and assemble all the Jews who are in Susa; fast on my behalf, all of you, not eating or drinking, night or day, for three days. I and my maids will also fast in the same way. Thus prepared, I will go to the king, contrary to the law. If I perish, I perish!" 17Mordecai went away and did exactly as Esther had commanded.

Through her faithful messenger, Esther begins a dialogue with Mordecai. She is reluctant to go to the king, fearing death for appearing before him unsummoned. She may also remember the consequences of Vashti's disobedience. Her own relationship with the king may be cooling. He has not sent for her in a month. It also seems that she has not fully realized the danger to herself. Her awareness of her Jewish heritage seems to have faded; her world is the world of the palace.

Mordecai is not deterred by Esther's fear nor will he allow her to ignore her own Jewish roots. With strong words he exhorts her to act. He reminds her that she faces death in any case: death for approaching the king or death as a Jew if she does not approach him. His final word is a testimony to divine providence: "Who knows but that it was for a time like this that you obtained the royal dignity?" Esther is not queen for her own sake; God has raised her to this position in order to use her as a savior of her people. In this she is reminiscent of Joseph who, as he says, was sold into slavery and raised to high position in order to be the savior of many people (Gen 50:20). If she fails, God will not be deterred. God will save the people; it is Esther who will perish.

Mordecai's words persuade Esther. At this moment she takes charge of her own destiny. She will accept the task set before her. She begins her preparation by declaring her intent to fast and asking for the supportive fast of all her people. She faces the possibility of death with courage. At this moment she becomes truly a queen.

ESTHER'S PRAYER

Esther C:12-30

12Queen Esther, seized with mortal anguish, likewise had recourse to the LORD. 13Taking off her splendid garments, she put on garments of distress and mourning. In place of her precious ointments she covered her head with dirt and ashes. She afflicted her body severely; all her festive adornments were put aside, and her hair was wholly disheveled.

[14]Then she prayed to the LORD, the God of Israel, saying: "My LORD, our King, you alone are God. Help me, who am alone and have no help but you, [15]for I am taking my life in my hand. [16]As a child I was wont to hear from the people of the land of my forefathers that you, O LORD, chose Israel from among all peoples, and our fathers from among all their ancestors, as a lasting heritage, and that you fulfilled all your promises to them. [17]But now we have sinned in your sight, and you have delivered us into the hands of our enemies, [18]because we worshiped their gods. You are just, O LORD. [19]But now they are not satisfied with our bitter servitude, but have undertaken [20]to do away with the decree you have pronounced, and to destroy your heritage; to close the mouths of those who praise you, and to extinguish the glory of your temple and your altar; [21]to open the mouths of the heathen to acclaim their false gods, and to extol an earthly king forever.

[22]"O LORD, do not relinquish your scepter to those that are nought. Let them not gloat over our ruin, but turn their own counsel against them and make an example of our chief enemy. [23]Be mindful of us, O LORD. Manifest yourself in the time of our distress and give me courage, King of gods and Ruler of every power. [24]Put in my mouth persuasive words in the presence of the lion, and turn his heart to hatred for our enemy, so that he and those who are in league with him may perish. [25]Save us by your power, and help me, who am alone and have no one but you, O LORD.

"You know all things. [26]You know that I hate the glory of the pagans, and abhor the bed of the uncircumcised or of any foreigner. [27]You know that I am under constraint, that I abhor the sign of grandeur which rests on my head when I appear in public; abhor it like a polluted rag, and do not wear it in private. [28]I, your handmaid, have never eaten at the table of Haman, nor have I graced the banquet of the king or drunk the wine of libations. [29]From the day I was brought here till now, your handmaid has had no joy except in you, O LORD, God of Abraham. [30]O God, more powerful

than all, hear the voice of those in despair. Save us from the
power of the wicked, and deliver me from my fear."

The content of Esther's prayer is found only in the Greek
additions, which expand the Hebrew story and make explicit
its veiled references to God.

The queen, who had attempted to dissuade Mordecai from
his penitential display, now herself puts on sackcloth and
ashes and begins to pray. She interweaves the traditional elements of a lament. She addresses her cry directly to God, who
alone can help her. She describes her distress: "I am taking my
life in my hand." She praises God: "You are just, O LORD." She
tries to motivate God to act: "You, O LORD, chose Israel from
among all peoples." She begs God to help her: "Save us from
the power of the wicked, and deliver me from my fear." The
whole prayer is a testimony to her faith and to her recognition
that all power belongs to God.

She persuades God with a reminder of God's faithfulness
to Israel in past ages and acknowledges God's justice in sending the people into exile. She is certain, however, that the total
extermination of the covenant people is not God's desire. So
she persuades further. If God allows the destruction of the
Jews, God will be surrendering power to an earthly ruler. She
underlines her point with the titles, "King of gods and Ruler
of every power." Then she returns to her petition that God,
who alone can help her, will give her the weapon of persuasive words.

Finally she focuses on herself. She declares her worthiness
to act as God's minister in this act of salvation. She has been
faithful to her Jewish tradition; she does not glory in the pomp
of the court. Her only joy is in God. Her prayer ends with a
third petition: "hear . . . save . . . deliver me from my fear."

AT RISK OF HER LIFE

Esther D

[1]On the third day, putting an end to her prayers, she took off
her penitential garments and arrayed herself in her royal attire. [2]In making her state appearance, after invoking the all-
seeing God and savior, she took with her two maids; [3]on the

one she leaned gently for support, 4while the other followed her, bearing her train. 5She glowed with the perfection of her beauty and her countenance was as joyous as it was lovely, though her heart was shrunk with fear. 6She passed through all the portals till she stood face to face with the king, who was seated on his royal throne, clothed in full robes of state, and covered with gold and precious stones, so that he inspired great awe. 7As he looked up, his features ablaze with the height of majestic anger, the queen staggered, changed color, and leaned weakly against the head of the maid in front of her. 8But God changed the king's anger to gentleness. In great anxiety he sprang from his throne, held her in his arms until she recovered, and comforted her with reassuring words. 9"What is it, Esther?" he said to her. "I am your brother. Take courage! 10You shall not die because of this general decree of ours. 11Come near!" 12Raising the golden scepter, he touched her neck with it, embraced her, and said, "Speak to me."

13She replied: "I saw you, my lord, as an angel of God, and my heart was troubled with fear of your majesty. 14For you are awesome, my lord, though your glance is full of kindness." 15As she said this, she fainted. 16The king became troubled and all his attendants tried to revive her.

Esther 5

1[Now on the third day, Esther put on her royal garments and stood in the inner courtyard, looking toward the royal palace, while the king was seated on his royal throne in the audience chamber, facing the palace doorway. 2He saw Queen Esther standing in the courtyard, and made her welcome by extending toward her the golden staff which he held. She came up to him, and touched the top of the staff.]

3Then the king said to her, "What is it, Queen Esther? What is your request? Even if it is half of my kingdom, it shall be granted you." 4"If it please your majesty," Esther replied, "come today with Haman to a banquet I have prepared." 5And the king ordered, "Have Haman make haste to fulfill the wish of Esther."

So the king went with Haman to the banquet Esther had prepared. 6During the drinking of the wine, the king said to Esther, "Whatever you ask for shall be granted, and whatever request you make shall be honored, even if it is for half my kingdom." [7]Esther replied: "This is my petition and request: [8]if I have found favor with the king and if it pleases your majesty to grant my petition and honor my request, come with Haman tomorrow to a banquet which I shall prepare for you; and then I will do as you ask."

The enhancement of the book made by the Greek additions can be clearly seen by comparing D:1-15 with 5:1-5, the story of Esther's approach to the king. In the Hebrew version (5:1-5) Esther, dressed in her royal garments, is simply welcomed by the king when he sees her approach. In the Greek version (D:1-15) the encounter has been made much more dramatic through a series of comparisons and contrasts. Esther's penitential garments are replaced by her royal attire. She appeals to God before going to appeal to the king. The beauty of Esther's face compares to the regal splendor of the king's appearance. The fire of the king's rage contrasts with the queen's pallor. God comes to Esther's rescue by changing the king's anger to gentleness.

The Hebrew version continues with the conversation between the king and Esther. She does not ask half the kingdom as the king suggests, nor does she ask for the rescue of her people. She simply invites the king to come with Haman to a banquet. The simplicity of her request veils the seriousness of her purpose. She carries out God's mission of saving the people, not by military exploits or prophetic preaching, but through the typical feminine means of an invitation to a meal.

At the first banquet which Esther prepares for the king and Haman (5:5-8), the king swears a second time to grant whatever Esther wishes, even half the kingdom. She requests only that the two men come to a second banquet. The delay serves the dramatic purpose of heightening the tension. We are left to wonder if Esther has lost her nerve, if she is testing the king's devotion to her, if she is waiting for Haman to make a foolish move. There is no answer; we, too, must wait for the second banquet.

Between the banquets the conflict between Mordecai and Haman intensifies (5:9–6:14). Haman's volatile nature is revealed by violent mood swings. He is puffed up by the invitation to the

queen's second banquet; he is distraught over Mordecai's repeated refusal to honor him. His wife suggests that he prepare a
giant gibbet (about seventy-five feet high) and ask the king to
have Mordecai hanged (or impaled) on it. This restores his good
humor, but his troubles are not over.

That same night the king, unable to sleep, has the royal
chronicles read to him. He hears the story of Mordecai's report
of the plot against the king (cf. 2:19-23) and discovers that
nothing has been done for Mordecai. So the next day he asks
Haman how a loyal servant should be rewarded. Haman,
thinking that the king is speaking of him, describes a public
display of honor. The king sends him out to honor Mordecai
according to his description. A humiliated Haman tells his
troubles to his wife who predicts that he will be defeated by
Mordecai. In this sorry state of mind he sets out for the second
banquet with the king and queen.

ESTHER'S REQUEST

Esther 7:1-8

1So the king and Haman went to the banquet with Queen
Esther. 2Again, on this second day, during the drinking of
the wine, the king said to Esther, "Whatever you ask, Queen
Esther, shall be granted you. Whatever request you make
shall be honored, even for half the kingdom." 3Queen Esther
replied: "If I have found favor with you, O king, and if it
pleases your majesty, I ask that my life be spared, and I beg
that you spare the lives of my people. 4For my people and I
have been delivered to destruction, slaughter, and extinc-
tion. If we were to be sold into slavery I would remain silent,
but as it is, the enemy will be unable to compensate for the
harm done to the king." 5"Who and where," said King
Ahasuerus to Queen Esther, "is the man who has dared to
do this?" 6Esther replied, "The enemy oppressing us is this
wicked Haman." At this, Haman was seized with dread of
the king and queen.

7The king left the banquet in anger and went into the garden
of the palace, but Haman stayed to beg Queen Esther for his
life, since he saw that the king had decided on his doom.
8When the king returned from the garden of the palace to
the banquet hall, Haman had thrown himself on the couch

on which Esther was reclining; and the king exclaimed,
"Will he also violate the queen while she is with me in my
own house!" Scarcely had the king spoken when the face of
Haman was covered over.

At the second banquet the king repeats the offer he made
at the first banquet: "Whatever you ask, Queen Esther, shall be
granted you." This is now the third time that the king has offered Esther as much as half the kingdom. Finally Esther presents her petition: "I ask that my life be spared, and I beg that
you spare the lives of my people." She adds the observation
that the slaughter of her people will do irreparable harm to the
king himself.

The king is astounded and demands to know the name of
the enemy who plans to do this dreadful thing. Esther names
Haman, who is overcome by dread. He has fatally underestimated the strength of those whom he planned to destroy. This
folly will mean his own destruction.

Haman thinks he has only one chance to escape death. He
appeals to the one whom he recognizes as most powerful with
the king, Esther. The method of his appeal, however, seals his
fate. The king sees his prostrate form on Esther's couch, not as
desperate submission, but as the threat of rape: "Will he also
violate the queen while she is with me in my own house!"[3]
Haman's indiscretion removes all hope; his face is described
as "covered over," as if he were already dead.

REVERSALS

Esther 7:9–8:12

[9]Harbona, one of the eunuchs who attended the king, said,
"At the house of Haman stands a gibbet fifty cubits high.
Haman prepared it for Mordecai, who gave the report that
benefited the king." The king answered, "Hang him on it."
[10]So they hanged Haman on the gibbet which he had made
ready for Mordecai, and the anger of the king abated.

[8:1]That day King Ahasuerus gave the house of Haman, enemy
of the Jews, to Queen Esther; and Mordecai was admitted to

---

[3]The verb *kabash*, here translated "violate" also means "rape."

the king's presence, for Esther had revealed his relationship to her. ²The king removed his signet ring from Haman, and transferred it into the keeping of Mordecai; and Esther put Mordecai in charge of the house of Haman.

³In another audience with the king, Esther fell at his feet and tearfully implored him to revoke the harm done by Haman the Agagite, and the plan he had devised against the Jews. ⁴The king stretched forth the golden scepter to Esther. So she rose and, standing in his presence, ⁵said: "If it pleases your majesty and seems proper to you, and if I have found favor with you and you love me, let a document be issued to revoke the letters which that schemer Haman, son of Hammedatha the Agagite, wrote for the destruction of the Jews in all the royal provinces. ⁶For how can I witness the evil that is to befall my people, and how can I behold the destruction of my race?"

⁷King Ahasuerus then said to Queen Esther and to the Jew Mordecai: "Now that I have given Esther the house of Haman, and they have hanged him on the gibbet because he attacked the Jews, ⁸you in turn may write in the king's name what you see fit concerning the Jews and seal the letter with the royal signet ring." For whatever is written in the name of the king and sealed with the royal signet ring cannot be revoked.

⁹At that time, on the twenty-third day of the third month, Sivan, the royal scribes were summoned. Exactly as Mordecai dictated, they wrote to the Jews and to the satraps, governors, and officials of the hundred and twenty-seven provinces from India to Ethiopia: to each province in its own script and to each people in its own language, and to the Jews in their own script and language. ¹⁰These letters, which he wrote in the name of King Ahasuerus and sealed with the royal signet ring, he sent by mounted couriers riding thoroughbred royal steeds. ¹¹In these letters the king authorized the Jews in each and every city to group together and defend their lives, and to kill, destroy, wipe out, along with their wives and children, every armed group of any nation or province which should attack them, and to seize their goods as spoil ¹²throughout the provinces of King Ahasuerus, on a single day, the thirteenth of the twelfth month, Adar.

In his irrational anger against Mordecai, Haman has unwittingly prepared for his own execution. The king decrees that Haman be hanged on the gibbet which he had prepared for his enemy. His house is given to Esther; Mordecai replaces him as keeper of the king's signet ring. Through Esther's influence, the roles of Haman and Mordecai are completely reversed.

Esther's major purpose, however, is still not resolved. According to the story the royal decrees of Persia are irrevocable. Thus the decree to slaughter the Jews still stands, even after Haman is dead. So Esther risks a second approach to the king. After he has welcomed her, she unveils a plan to counteract the decree. The king continues to give Esther whatever she wishes. He empowers her to write a second irrevocable decree in his name and sealed with his signet ring. Mordecai dictates the new decree which authorizes the Jews to defend themselves against the slaughter commanded by the first decree.

Esther 9:11-15

11On the same day, when the number of those killed in the stronghold of Susa was reported to the king, 12he said to Queen Esther: "In the stronghold of Susa the Jews have killed and destroyed five hundred men, as well as the ten sons of Haman. What must they have done in the other royal provinces! You shall again be granted whatever you ask, and whatever you request shall be honored." 13So Esther said, "If it pleases your majesty, let the Jews in Susa be permitted again tomorrow to act according to today's decree, and let the ten sons of Haman be hanged on gibbets." 14The king then gave an order to this effect, and the decree was published in Susa. So the ten sons of Haman were hanged, 15and the Jews in Susa mustered again on the fourteenth of the month of Adar and killed three hundred men in Susa.

Still the story does not end. Once more the king promises Esther whatever she requests. Once more a decree is issued according to Esther's wishes, granting the Jews authority to defend themselves against their enemies. Once more Esther is the source of power for the people.

FEAST OF PURIM

Esther 9:24-32

24Haman, son of Hammedatha the Agagite, the foe of all the Jews, had planned to destroy them and had cast the *pur*, or lot, for the time of their defeat and destruction. 25Yet, when Esther entered the royal presence, the king ordered in writing that the wicked plan Haman had devised against the Jews should instead be turned against Haman and that he and his sons should be hanged on gibbets. 26And so these days have been named Purim after the word *pur*.

Thus, because of all that was contained in this letter, and because of what they had witnessed and experienced in this affair, 27the Jews established and took upon themselves, their descendants, and all who should join them, the inviolable obligation of celebrating these two days every year in the manner prescribed by this letter, and at the time appointed. 28These days were to be commemorated and kept in every generation, by every clan, in every province, and in every city. These days of Purim were never to fall into disuse among the Jews, nor into oblivion among their descendants.

29Queen Esther, daughter of Abihail and of Mordecai the Jew, wrote to confirm with full authority this second letter about Purim, 30when Mordecai sent documents concerning peace and security to all the Jews in the hundred and twenty-seven provinces of Ahasuerus' kingdom. 31Thus were established, for their appointed time, these days of Purim which Mordecai the Jew and Queen Esther had designated for the Jews, just as they had previously enjoined upon themselves and upon their race the duty of fasting and supplication. 32The command of Esther confirmed these prescriptions for Purim and was recorded in the book.

In this chapter the story of Esther is used to explain the foundation of the Jewish festival of Purim. Just as the spring rituals of non-Israelite farmers and shepherds were given a historical context and shaped into the festival of Passover in order to memorialize God's deliverance of the people at the exodus, so also the Babylonian festival celebrating the reversal of fates at the New Year is given a Jewish story in order to memorialize God's salvation of the good (Mordecai) and punishment of the wicked (Haman). The Babylonian word *puru-um*, meaning "lot" or "fate," becomes the Hebrew word Purim, "lots." The name of the feast, Purim, is then connected to Haman's casting of lots to determine the date for the slaughter of the Jews.

The Jewish festival of Purim is celebrated on the fourteenth to fifteenth of the month of Adar (February-March), the last month of the Jewish calendar.[4] It is a minor feast, introduced into the calendar long after the major feasts of Passover, Pentecost, and Tabernacles. The festival is characterized by loud and sometimes rowdy celebration. The Talmud says participants may drink until they cannot distinguish between the shouted statements: "Blessed be Mordecai" and "Cursed be Haman." In medieval times the story of Esther and Mordecai was often dramatized. Children in Israel today dress in costume and beg for little gifts of money, a custom similar to that of American children on Halloween.

Esther, identified as queen and as the biological daughter of Abihail and the adopted daughter of Mordecai, is portrayed as the authority who promulgates the celebration of Purim. She and Mordecai establish the proper days and practices for the feast.

SAVIOR OF HER PEOPLE

Esther F

[1]Then Mordecai said: "This is the work of God. [2]I recall the dream I had about these very things, and not a single detail has been left unfulfilled—[3]the tiny spring that grew into a river, the light of the sun, the many waters. The river is Esther, whom the king married and made queen. [4]The two dragons are myself and Haman. [5]The nations are those who assembled to destroy the name of the Jews, [6]but my people is Israel, who cried to God and was saved.

[4]Because the Jewish calendar is based on lunar months, an extra month is added every few years in order to keep the calendar synchronized with the solar year. The extra month is Adar Sheni (second Adar), added at the end of the year. In such leap years Purim is celebrated in the month of Adar Sheni.

"The LORD saved his people and delivered us from all these evils. God worked signs and great wonders, such as have not occurred among the nations. ⁷For this purpose he arranged two lots: one for the people of God, the second for all the other nations. ⁸These two lots were fulfilled in the hour, the time, and the day of judgment before God and among all the nations. ⁹God remembered his people and rendered justice to his inheritance.

¹⁰"Gathering together with joy and happiness before God, they shall celebrate these days on the fourteenth and fifteenth of the month Adar throughout all future generations of his people Israel."

¹⁴[Postscript] In the fourth year of the reign of Ptolemy and Cleopatra, Dositheus, who said he was a priest and Levite, and his son Ptolemy brought the present letter of Purim, saying that it was genuine and that Lysimachus, son of Ptolemy, of the community of Jerusalem, had translated it.

There is a final Greek addition to the Book of Esther which, like the first addition, describes a dream of Mordecai. In the first description of the dream (A:4-10), Mordecai sees two dragons poised for mortal combat. The battle of these two enemies threatens the just people of the world with destruction. When the just cry out to God, a little spring becomes a great river. The sun comes out and the lowly devour those who are honored. Mordecai's dream is interpreted in the final Greek addition (F:1-10). The little spring which becomes a great river is Esther, the queen. Her becoming great is the beginning of the salvation of the people.

The story of Esther is the story of a beautiful young Jewish woman who is raised to great power. Initially she is passive, accepting the instructions and guidance of others, submitting to whatever is expected of her. The threatened destruction of her people is the crisis which brings her to full development. She heeds the words of her adoptive father and mentor Mordecai: "Who knows but that it was for a time like this that you obtained the royal dignity?" The full strength of her character appears in her courageous approach to the king to plead for her people. The depth of her wisdom is revealed in her patient arrangement of circumstances which will assure her of a favorable answer from the king. At the end of the story she has reached her full power as a faithful Jewish woman and the Persian queen. She exercises both political and liturgical authority. Through her, God has once again restored the life of the covenant people.

Bibliography

Bach, Alice, ed. *The Pleasure of Her Text: Feminist Readings of Biblical and Historical Texts.* Philadelphia: Trinity Press International, 1990.

Bellis, Alice O. *Helpmates, Harlots, Heroes: Women's Stories in The Hebrew Bible.* Louisville, Ky.: Westminster/John Knox, 1994.

Brenner, Athalya. *The Israelite Woman: Social Role and Literary Type in Biblical Narrative.* Sheffield: JSOT, 1985.

Darr, Kathryn Pfisterer. *Far More Precious Than Jewels: Perspectives on Biblical Women.* Gender and the Biblical Tradition; Louisville, Ky.: Westminster/John Knox, 1991.

Day, Peggy L., ed. *Gender and Difference in Ancient Israel.* Minneapolis: Fortress, 1989.

LaCocque, André. *The Feminine Unconventional: Four Subversive Figures in Israel's Tradition.* Overtures to Biblical Theology; Minneapolis: Fortress, 1990.

McKenna, Megan. *Not Counting Women and Children.* Maryknoll, Orbis, 1994.

Newsom, Carol A., and Sharon H. Ringe, eds. *The Women's Bible Commentary.* Louisville, Ky.: Westminster/John Knox, 1992.

Nunnally-Cox, J. Ellen. *Foremothers: Women of the Bible.* San Francisco: Harper & Row, 1981.

O'Connor, Kathleen M. *The Wisdom Literature.* Message of Biblical Spirituality 5; Wilmington, Del.: Michael Glazier, 1988.

Sleevi, Mary Lou. *Women of the Word.* Notre Dame, Ind.: Ave Maria, 1989.

Trible, Phyllis. *God and the Rhetoric of Sexuality.* Overtures to Biblical Theology; Philadelphia: Fortress, 1978.

_____. *Texts of Terror: Literary-Feminist Readings of Biblical Narratives.* Overtures to Biblical Theology; Philadelphia: Fortress, 1984.

Winter, Miriam Therese. *WomanWisdom.* New York: Crossroad, 1991.

_____. *WomanWitness.* New York: Crossroad, 1992.